Self-
Devouring
Growth

A PLANETARY PARABLE

AS TOLD FROM SOUTHERN AFRICA

Julie Livingston

DUKE UNIVERSITY PRESS
Durham and London
2019

© 2019 Duke University Press
All rights reserved
Printed in the United States of America on
acid-free paper ∞
Designed by Amy Ruth Buchanan
Typeset in Arno by
Tseng Information Systems, Inc.

Cataloging-in-Publication Data is available from the Library of Congress.

ISBN 9781478005087 (hard cover : alk. paper)
ISBN 9781478006398 (pbk. : alk. paper)
ISBN 9781478007005 (ebook)

Cover art: James Cullinane, *Rain Drawing* 2, 2017.
Ink and acrylic on panel, 12 × 9 in. Courtesy of the artist
and Robert Henry Contemporary, New York.

FOR HAZEL

CONTENTS

ACKNOWLEDGMENTS

This little book has been buoyed by an ocean of generosity. My gratitude is deep, expansive, and heartfelt for all those who carried it, and me, along. Most significantly, I owe an enormous debt to the many people over the years in Botswana who gently, patiently, wedged open spaces in my imagination for new worlds to grow.

The book began as a lecture written for the Johannesburg Workshop in Theory and Criticism (JWTC). I am grateful to the organizers: Julia Hornberger, Zen Marie, Achille Mbembe, and Dhammamegha Leat for the invitation and thought-provoking workshop, and to my fellow JWTC 2015 participants (especially Anne Allison, Kaushik Sunder Rajan, and Behrooz Ghamari-Tabrizi) for encouragement and ideas. Ghassan Hage will see how his own paper planted a seed that grew. I am deeply indebted to Catherine Burns, who not only asked terrific questions in Johannesburg but also took good care of me when I was ailing. Toby Jones and Megan Vaughan each read early drafts of that lecture (which became chapter 1), sharpening my thinking enormously and encouraging me to continue.

Drafts of chapter 2 were developed as part of a series of meetings organized by Abou Farman and Richard Rottenburg. I am so grateful to both of them and to the other members of the Measures of Future Health group — Miriam Ticktin, Susan Erickson, Sandra Calk, Vincent DuClos, and Celia Lowe — for asking all the right questions across multiple drafts, and for their superb scholarship that sets me thinking. I am especially grateful to Abou for the careful editorial advice.

In addition to the JWTC and Measures of Future Health, I benefited enormously from the patience, intelligence, and generosity of many audiences where I tried out various parts of the manuscript: the Anthropology Department at Stanford, the Anthropology Department at University of Michigan, the Anthropology Department at Duke, the Department of the History of Medicine at Johns Hopkins, the Discard Studies Group at New York University (NYU), the Colloquium Series on Shifting Social Contracts in Postcolonial Governance at The New School, the Anthropology Department at the University of Amsterdam, the Anthropology Department at Brown, the Ifriqiyya Colloquium at Columbia, the History Department at Columbia, the MacArthur Fellows Forum, the Seminar in Global Health at Princeton, the Epicentre workshop on Configuring Contagion in Biosocial Epidemics at Aarhus University, the History Department at NYU, the Department of the History and Sociology of Science at the University of Pennsylvania, the Department of Social and Cultural Analysis at NYU, and the Anthropology Department at NYU. I am particularly grateful to Bruce Grant, Victoria Koski-Karrell, Elizabeth Roberts, Scott Stonington, Antina von Schnitzler, Adriana Petryna, Joao Biehl, Carolyn Rouse, Rijk Van Dyck, Lisa Stevenson, Lotte Meinart, Lynn Thomas, Dean Saranillo, Gil Anidjar, Zenia Kish, Dilshanie Perera, Jess Auerbach, AnneMaria Makhulu, Charlie Piot, Randy Matory, Vivian Lu, Dean Chahim, Lana Povitz, Nuala Caomhanach, Lochlann Jain, Harris Solomon, Mana Kia, and Mamadou Diouf for their thoughtful comments and questions.

At NYU I am fortunate indeed for the presence of so many smart, creative, and hilarious faculty and staff in the Department of Social and Cultural Analysis and the History Department. In particular I thank my co-teacher Thuy Linh Tu who taught me more than I could possibly hope for when we taught "Strategies" together. (Someone ring the bell, I said Strategies.)

Many of the ideas here took me back to discussions in graduate school with one of my most beloved mentors, the late Ivan Karp. My debt to him is enormous. So many thanks to Mike McGovern, who since our time in graduate school has consistently set the standard for how to carry the very best of those concepts we learned forward, and to Randy Packard for teaching me to pay careful attention to political economy even when it was unfashionable. Other ideas were born during a collaborative project with Jasbir Puar. I hope Jasbir can see her genius lurking here, and the grounding I get from our many years of conversation. Still other ideas began in Gaborone in 2007 amid conversations and debates with Patrick Monnaesi and Betsey Brada. *Ke a leboga ditsala tsa me.*

While writing this book I was immensely lucky to work very closely with some of the most marvelous graduate students: Tyler Zoanni, Steven Thrasher, Emma Shaw Crane, Sunaura Taylor, Laura Philips, Andrew Seaton, and Emily Lim Rogers. Each of them gives me badly needed hope for this world. I trust Sunaura Taylor and Emma Shaw Crane will see how much they taught me and how the conversations begun in our respective directed readings have stayed with me. Emily Lim Rogers deserves special thanks for hunting down images and permissions, and helping me think through options with great patience. Participants in my 2018 Interspecies Seminar — Justin Linds, Emily Lim Rogers, Faith McGlothlin, Nuala Caomanach, Tanvi Kapoor, Sam Prendergast, Tristan Beach, Katherine McLeod, Lukas La Rivière, Leandra Barrett, Daryl Meador, Laura Murray, Katherine Sinclair, Zeynep Oguz, and Brittany Haynes — opened up so many new ideas, while reminding me of the joys of thinking together.

As someone whose mind at times — and despite my best intentions — has a tendency to swim in dark waters, and whose body often gives way at inopportune moments, I depend on my brilliant friends to guide me toward the light and keep me safe and well. At various moments as this book took shape Behrooz Ghamari-Tabrizi, Jasbir Puar, Nicole Fleetwood, Thuy Linh Tu, Zoe Wool, Kris Peterson, Sherine Hamdy, Jennifer Morgan, Herman Bennett, Nikhil Singh, Annika Tamura, Marikka Tamura, Lynn Thomas, Lotte Meinart, Megan Vaughan, Audrey Bedolis, Louise Gore, Ed Cohen, Anne Hubbell, Jennifer Cole, David Schoenbrun, Gary Wilder, Elly Truitt, Elaine Freedgood, Stephanie Cohen, Adam Keats, Vincanne Adams, and Stacey Langwick have offered their clarity, inspiration, and irreverence and kept me going. A million thanks to Shannon Green—the ultimate body-genius—for her steadying presence in my life.

In great feats of generosity, Vincanne Adams, Pierre Du-Plessis, Deborah Durham, Behrooz Ghamari-Tabrizi, Kris Peterson (my rescue cow!), and Andrew Ross read the entire manuscript with great insight and provided me with vital feedback. *Ke a leboga thata* (a gazillion thatas) to Jackie Solway, who, in addition to reading the whole book and saving me from numerous errors of fact and interpretation, also generously gave me many of the photographs used here. I am particularly thankful to Anna Tsing, and an anonymous reviewer who offered detailed comments and that invaluable gift—encouragement.

I am deeply grateful to the John D. and Catherine T. MacArthur Foundation, and especially to Cecilia Conrad and Marlies Carruth for their ongoing support, and invitation to try new things. A residency at the University of Washington's Whitely Center and a fellowship at the Mesa Refuge for Writers offered me space to think and write far away from the concrete of Manhattan, for which I am ever thankful. I am especially indebted to Peter Barnes and Susan Page Tillet of Mesa Refuge, and to Bob Friedman who supported my fellowship there. At Mesa Refuge I hit the jackpot with two amazing fellow-writer housemates, Brandon Keim and Susan Ochshorn. Conversations with Brandon, ever curious and patient lover of all creatures carried me over the finish line.

I know how fortunate I am to have Ken Wissoker as my editor. Having him and Cathy Davidson in New York City now just makes it all the better. I am grateful to Ken, Joshua Tranen, Liz Smith, and the staff at Duke University Press for the care they bring to their work and to Jehanne Moharram for such expert copyediting. Thank goodness there are still books in this world.

This book is dedicated to Hazel, whom I love so much. Though she is coming of age in these troubling times, I take comfort in the fact that she is one of the strongest people I know.

Upon my return at the end of a long trip I like to listen to Sibelius's *En Saga*. As the music plays, I feel the burdens of the journey falling away even as I unwind its transformative moments and stow them carefully away. So too, it seems, at the end of a book, especially one imagined as a parabolic journey. Behrooz gave me this piece of music, and as with all his gifts, my life would be so impoverished without it. It is nearly impossible for me to imagine having written this book without such a beautiful mind to dialogue with or such a beautiful soul to inspire me and keep me close. He has read every word, and more than once. It was he, I believe, who first came up with the term "self-devouring growth." Like all things he touches, this book and its author are better for his love and care.

A Planetary Parable

If growth automatically generated well-being, we would now be
living in a paradise. We are in fact going down the road to hell.
–Serge Latouche, *Farewell to Growth*

Pathological consumption has become so normalized
that we scarcely notice it.
–George Monbiot, *The Gift of Death*

There is no end
To what a living world
Will demand of you.
–Lauren Olamina,
Earthseed: The Books of the Living

THIS LITTLE BOOK CONTAINS a parable of sorts about
self-devouring growth, a term I use to refer to the ways
that the super-organism of human beings is consuming
itself. This is not a new tale. Many others have offered their versions over the years.[1] But like all parables, the lessons are worth
contemplating anew.[2] The story is told from Botswana, southern
Africa's miracle land, but self-devouring growth is everywhere to
be seen. Wherever you sit reading this you are in a world organized by self-devouring growth. It is so fundamental as to be unremarkable, and yet it is eating away at the very ground beneath
our feet. Whether you are a Motswana or someone who has
never set foot in southern Africa such that the details of this particular version of the story are new to you, the plotlines should
be familiar as they are yours and mine as well.[3]

Parable is a realist genre. What is to follow is not merely allegory. But parables also have larger meanings that are revealed through their structure as "illustrative parallel" or extended metaphor. Perhaps it is helpful to know that parable and parabola share a common root.[4] In a parable we travel out, unfolding the metaphor in a parabolic shape. By journey's end, we will have returned to the same plane on which we started, but somewhat farther along, in the hopes of having learned something from our experience along the way. In this case we will follow three metaphors in sequence. Each of them is material in nature. Each has a thingyness one can touch, see, smell, hear. Parables reveal urgent and sometimes uncomfortable truths that are hiding in plain sight.[5] They conjoin the listener (and in this case the teller as well!) to recognize herself within the story. As your narrator, my use of the word "we" is not accidental. I have located myself at various moments in this account. So can you.

Botswana offers as fine a protagonist as any for this tale, which necessarily journeys at times to other lands. I have chosen her as our central character in this parable because I know her well and love her dearly, not because she is somehow more misguided than others. Far from it. Botswana is an upper-middle-income country, a "developing" country, in fact a paradigmatically successful one. She's never gone to war. The modern nation of Botswana was born poor but peaceful amid a devastating drought. She came of age in a tough neighborhood surrounded by the violence and greed of institutionalized racism on all sides. Yet since gaining independence from Great Britain in 1966, Botswana has undergone decades of spectacular postcolonial economic growth, though things have leveled off of late. Out of the diamonds found secreted in her rock, the country has built schools and a system of universal health care, telecommunications and roads, clean water and pensions, vast nature preserves, and a functioning democracy. Of course, there was a time when human society was structured in such a way that nature preserves and old-age pensions were unnecessary. That does not take away from this impressive and vital postcolonial achievement, and the skill and intelligence of the people behind it. But it does remind us that industrial modernity is only one way to live.

ecological sin?

Botswana is widely regarded as a developmental success, a miracle even.[6] But even that success, it seems, presents its own uncertainties, its own horizon as growth becomes self-devouring. This growth has become the organizing logic of her development, its hoped-for future. And yet insatiable growth predicated on consumption will inevitably overwhelm.[7] Botswana is a place from which we can think about the telos of development in relation to what the pope is calling "ecological sin."

Botswana forces difficult questions onto the table; the moral of the story is not a simple one. The signs on the ground at present are anxious ones; we should divine their truths with great care. The future is always uncertain; no one knows what lies ahead. Sometimes dire scientific prophecies fail to materialize as forecast. Sometimes destruction comes out of seemingly nowhere and catches everyone by surprise. Scientific predictions of African environmental collapse have a long and troubling history. This is because scientific authority has been used to blame African practices for environmental challenges from desertification to ebola. Yet upon closer examination these problems arise out of complex political and economic histories rooted in European colonialism and/or corporate capitalism.[8] My parable is not anti-science, this would be a false move. While its predictions need to be understood as provisional, a welter of scientific observation underpins the stories that lie ahead.

In 2016 record-breaking temperatures reached 44 degrees Celsius in the town of Maun in Botswana's northern Okavango region, and over 43 degrees in other parts of the country. If global temperatures continue to climb in the ways scientists predict, Botswana will be one of the many places that will have more days of extreme heat, with predicted increases in heat-related deaths, an upsurge in malaria and dengue fever (diseases that were historically absent, except for endemic malaria in Okavango), and increasing drought, with attendant food and water insecurity.[9] Grassland pasture is giving way to thornbush. The water table is sinking. Scientists predict that the wild painted dogs and the elusive antbear will die out in this shifting ecology. They caution that the spectacular Okavango Delta—the hub of Botswana's high-end eco-tourism industry, the nation's second largest in-

climate change

come earner, and site of some of the earliest human societies—will lose biodiversity as flooding and water distribution patterns shift and the water table drops. The day will eventually arrive when the diamonds that propelled Botswana's climb out of poverty are finished. The predictions are so dire that many either turn away in fatalism or dismiss them as exaggeration. Wherever we look, anticipating disasters now drives its own kind of growth industry.[10] What if the end is nigh, but for a major rethinking and reorientation of human activity?

What were Batswana (as the people of Botswana call themselves) to do but grow their economy as best they could when the British left them deeply impoverished, and proletarianized, on a planet already polluted and warming through no fault of Batswana themselves?[11] Batswana have managed their development trajectory quite well—and yet, as you will read in the story that follows, all this and more may be in jeopardy in the coming years. Climate change and environmental conditions have long been part of a national conversation in Botswana, where technical expertise in conservation, agriculture, and geology is deep and authoritative. And yet . . . setting this story in Botswana will help elucidate our planetary predicament—an existential crisis if there ever was one, for those who live in the interstices of what are often narrated as the great political and economic divides of the contemporary world—rich/poor; first world/third world; north/south. A caution is perhaps in order for my fellow American readers—before you think you know what's best for Botswana, you might consider the dynamics of growth in California.

The Problem of Self-Devouring Growth

Economic growth is a paradigm that has become so second nature that when people are thinking about a place in this world and how to improve it, immediately they/we assume that growth must be the basis of that effort. Without us really noticing it, growth has become this unmarked category granted magical powers. As growth remains the common sense, the unexamined imperative, and so much is done in its name, a cascade of

[margin handwritten note: growth should NOT be the Basis]

unseen consequences, side effects, also become second nature, a process I call self-devouring growth.

Self-devouring growth is a name for a set of material relationships. By material I mean there is something with physical properties being devoured. Growth is not inherently bad. Growth can be healthy, can be a sign of vitality. Self-devouring growth departs from these other forms by operating under an imperative—grow or die; grow or be eaten—with an implicit assumption that this growth is predicated on uninhibited consumption. The perversion happens in two linked ways: first in how the protagonists of growth envision and appropriate the resources upon which it is fed, and second in how they attend to the production of waste that is a by-product of consumption-driven growth. This particular model of growth even became a logical means of constructing healthy, robust societies, such that there is something intractable about this thinking—grow the economy, grow a business, grow a market, grow, grow, GROW! is a mantra so powerful that it obscures the destruction it portends.[12]

In other words, self-devouring growth is a cancerous model. These are mutant forms of out-of-control growth that emerge in nodes but eventually spread into every crevice of the planetary body, harnessing its blood supply, eating through its tissue, producing rot and pain that will eventually kill the larger organism. As with cancer, we mourn each individual loss as tragic, be it Bob Marley, my Aunt Jill, the American bison, or the Guatemalan farmland now lying open as a suppurating wound after the Canadian-owned nickel mine consumed the bedrock. And yet the big picture of what is driving these losses is almost too big to take in. And so the larger dynamic of destruction is somehow accepted as the necessary cost of the good things in life.[13]

We pour our hopes into technological solutions. Technologies can be wonderful, but they are insufficient to save us from a problem whose roots lie deeper. Certainly electric cars are better than gasoline-powered cars. But if everyone is to have one, and if everyone is to want a new one every few years, we will still consume vast quantities of glass, aluminum, plastic, and steel, still have a problem of disposing of used tires and brake fluid, of building road capacity, of mining cobalt, nickel, lithium, and

[handwritten margin note: growth is destructive]

[handwritten note: technology as a beacon of hope]

graphite to power them. The capitalism that structures the contemporary global economy is the most significant engine of this dynamic, its organizing telos, and peddler of its narcotic. Ever more intensive forms of capitalist consumption animate a system that will harm everyone, even those whose consumption mainly remains aspirational. But while self-devouring growth is the central dynamic of capitalism, it cannot be reduced to it.[14] The former Soviet Union undertook its own version of self-devouring growth. So did Maoist China.

When later in this book we follow Botswana beef into a Norwegian primary school cafeteria — a Scandinavian socialist space if there ever was one — what we will find is nonetheless part of a larger system of growth-led planetary devastation that will happen long before the poor get their turn at the trough.[15] Despite some of the redistributions of socialism, consumption by the elite, middle class, and aspirant grows at rates that far outstrip these leveling forces, dictating a disposition toward growth without end. The underclass — standing there on the front lines as they always must do — may get little growth but be devoured nonetheless. Sir Richard Branson, airline magnate, and his "team" rode out Hurricane Irma in the well-stocked and fortified bunker on his private Caribbean island, while people in neighboring Barbuda (perhaps home to some of his "team") lacked such protections entirely. Recovery becomes its own growth industry.[16]

Some might object, as they have since Malthus, that population growth drives the need for economic growth and so it is the poor, those chronic reproducers, who must be tamed. Yet this is a misunderstanding of how consumption, not to mention reproduction, works. Take New York City, where I live, as an example. A recent report estimated that only 2 percent of the one million buildings in my city accounted for 45 percent of the city's energy use and attendant greenhouse gas emissions. These buildings included those where some of the wealthiest New Yorkers (Donald Trump, David Koch, Alice Walton — all climate-change deniers) reside. Meanwhile low- and middle-income New Yorkers, packed into tiny apartments and necessarily frugal about their energy use in our very expensive city, were nonetheless disproportionately exposed to the dangers of Hurricane Sandy. Over half of the victims of the storm surge were renters with average annual incomes of USD 18,000,[17] well below the city median of USD 60,000. Or consider the problem in regional terms. An average citizen of the United States like myself requires more than twice the amount of bioproductive space on our finite planet to support her consumption than the average European. The European, in turn, consumes twenty times the rate of most Africans.[18] While the elite consume the most and then the middle classes, these days even the poor consume at escalating rates. Yet they are sold poor-quality goods that make them ill, and are forced to reside amid the toxic detritus — the by-products and the wastelands of growth.[19]

Development is often posited as economic growth.[20] Under its umbrella there are many projects and visions for better health, education, and well-being, but these are often subsumed by the hegemonic growth vision of development economists. Arguments are made that health, education, infrastructure, and institutional capacity will all facilitate growth. Units of analysis in turn truncate and bind relationships of distribution, such that redistribution is left a national affair at best.[21] Proponents imagine growth as the way to ensure that the needs of the poor are taken care of. There is a sense that if everything grows then finally there will be enough. But this trickle-down fantasy will dry up as resource scarcity increases on our finite planet.

Meanwhile, up at the top and increasingly in the middle and even below, consumption escalates rapidly. Growth is said to bring jobs, but often it does not. Or the jobs arrive and then depart again never to return, or the jobs arrive, but they pay so little for work so numbing that they fail to be the ladders to the good life imagined by the growth proponents.[22] This is certainly the case in Botswana, where the economy has grown, the population has urbanized, and yet despite persistent effort, unemployment remains intractable. Botswana has placed nets underneath her poorest citizens, who like the poor everywhere are disproportionately female; it has sought pathways for many out of the poverty that the colonial migrant labor system wrought. These are incredibly important achievements. But Botswana has been unable to employ her people adequately in an economy structured around growth. Africa's miracle is the third most unequal country on the continent, the tenth most unequal on earth. The Gini coefficient tells as much about rampant consumption at the top, and increasingly in the middle, as it does about the poverty at the bottom. By 2015 the World Bank was cautioning that consumer spending, facilitated in large part on credit, was driving Botswana's economy.[23] The relationship between growth and personal debt is its own self-devouring paradox.

Is Another World Possible?

Growth-driven development is also predicated on a facile evolutionary model.[24] The implicit aim is to take Botswana or Honduras or Cambodia and, through economic growth, create infrastructure and consumption like there is in Canada or Australia. The same of course could be said for turning Brownsville, Brooklyn, into Park Slope. And yet, these developed economies that are the aspiration are the prime engines of a kind of voraciousness that is leading us off a cliff. Perhaps new goals are in order for Park Slope and Brownsville alike. Figuring out these goals will require understanding how Park Slope and Brownsville or, say, Honduras and Canada, are actually two sides of a single relationship. Figuring out these goals will also require a new imagination.

Over the past few centuries there have been forms of thought, modes of reasoning, and metaphysical understandings all over the world that were deemed irrational, superstitious, marginal, and whatever else under the sign of colonialism and enlightenment reason. But all our rational thought and rational knowledge — development, from economics to engineering being a good example — has produced a world that is highly irrational indeed over the long run, suicidal, self-devouring. What else might we find if we take seriously those forms of knowledge that have been purged or suppressed? I don't say any of this as a romantic gesture — replacing industrial (and postindustrial) capitalism and techno-science with nineteenth-century Tswana healing rites is neither tenable nor a plausible solution for what

Can't go back!

ails us.[25] But as we follow these tales, I will show you forms of insight, ethical modalities, metaphysical flashes of brilliance, and modes of life worth contemplating. Such knowledge can contribute to the unlocking of our collective imagination, an imagination we are going to need quite dearly in the rapidly unfolding future.

We aren't going back. We can't. And why would we want to? That would mean a world without insulin, and quite possibly amid that rapacious obscenity of self-devouring growth, the Atlantic slave trade. Relying on women and girls to carry water on their heads many kilometers each day is not a romantic vision. The point is not that things are worse now than they were then (though they may be for some), but rather that we may well be devouring our future. If we are to think beyond the self-devouring growth drive, then we must open those repositories of the imagination—the before, the against, and the besides—that have been or are now being crushed by it.[26] There are many of them. This book opens the storehouse in Botswana and reads from a few corners of a vast field of insight.[27]

The worlds therein are not utopian. Nor are these worlds homogenous or static. The territory of modern Botswana has been a place of dynamic human creativity longer than most other places on earth, though my story will be drawing from only a few centuries deep. Beginning in roughly 1400 CE, but picking up pace amid the droughts of the eighteenth century, groups of African settlers, who much later would be anachronistically referred to by historians as "Tswana," moved onto the eastern plateau (the highveld) of present-day Botswana.[28] Their large herds of cattle gave them a mode of claiming territorial sovereignty. The highveld was not empty when they arrived. Nor were these "Tswana" one people or one polity. Mixed societies of Bantu, San, and Khoe people already there fled west as the newcomers arrived, heading farther into the Kalahari Desert. Or if they stayed, they might have had their cattle seized, or their hunting and gathering curtailed, rendering them as cattle-herding servants or slaves for the new residents.

Over the ensuing centuries, refugees and other migrant groups would be incorporated into the growing kingdoms/

chiefdoms. Ecological stress or political tension caused new groups to splinter off and settle new areas. As historian Paul Landau tells us, these societies were "well-equipped to embrace and absorb strangers."[29] As such they were mixed and continually mixing, flexible and adaptive. The term "Tswana" used throughout my story hardens this fluidity and heterogeneity and thereby misleads. Absorption did not mean an erasure of origins. Hierarchies of origin and of genealogy mattered, as did those of gender and age. A whole welter of ethnic mythos, alternating between the romantic and the derogatory, emerged to characterize the ethnic underclasses and explain their oppressed status. The arrival of British missionaries and eventual colonization in the nineteenth century amplified such depictions while also consolidating a new ethnonym—Tswana. Among people there was debate, disagreement, and difference, there were struggles and tensions, much of which will necessarily be glossed over in the tale I will tell.

Though my story will efface some of this richness, it finds in Tswana thought and practice traces that suggest other politics by which distribution might proceed—amid a growth that is cyclical rather than relentless. Sometimes a cycle of growth was leveled through horrible experiences of collapse like famine, epidemic disease, or war. Such clues recall a place in which some property is collective and attendant responsibilities are assumed, yet managed through gendered and age-based hierarchies of access; polities that engage in participatory democracy amid palpable pecking orders of status and wealth and the private dealings they portend; people who prize autonomy but assume interdependence.

What follows will unfold in three parts: water, food, movement—all vital human needs. Or put another way, rain, cattle, roads—all distribution systems that are good to think with. There are others. One could tell a thousand and one tales of self-devouring growth, but I will limit myself to three.

water | food | movement
"rain | cattle | roads

1

Rainmaking and Other Forgotten Things

"Even the trees were dying, from the roots upward," he said.
"Does everything die like this?"

"No," she said. "You may see no rivers on the ground but we keep the
rivers inside us. That is why all good things and all good people are
called rain. Sometimes we see the rain clouds gather even though not
a cloud appears in the sky. It is all in our heart."

He nodded his head, fully grasping this in its deepest meaning. There
was always something on this earth man was forced to love and
worship by reason of its absence. People in cloudy, misty climates
worshipped the sun, and people in semi-desert
countries worshipped the rain.

–Bessie Head, *When Rain Clouds Gather*

ACROSS THE WORLD RIGHT NOW there is a crisis of water. The crisis takes many forms. In June 2015, a front-page article in the *New York Times* revealed that a third of the world's thirty-seven largest aquifers are being drained faster than they are being replenished.[1] The following year readers would learn that the water engineering firm contracted by city officials in Flint, Michigan, had drawn water with high chloride levels into the municipal system, thus corroding the pipes and poisoning the people of Flint with lead and other toxins, a situation that years later has not been remediated.[2]

Meanwhile, nearby, the Nestlé Corporation is drawing ground-water to bottle for sale.[3] This is a crisis in the sense that Janet Roitman describes—a form of the normal, named and felt as emergency so as to suggest a before and an after, when in fact the conditions of possibility are ongoing as they have been for some time.[4] This is a crisis of public health. Our entry point into this planetary crisis lies in southern Africa, in the increasingly thirsty nation of Botswana.

Water is a necessary precondition for growth. Without water there is no city. Agriculture, construction, mining, tourism, health care, manufacturing—all of these require significant quantities of water. Hence these water problems are global. They are also interconnected. The Veolia engineering firm, which is now being sued by residents of Flint, Michigan, has what they call "multi-local presence,"[5] with divisions around the world. That includes one in Botswana, which "has enjoyed rapid growth in the last several years."[6] Water flows underground and on the surface of our planet. It collects in lakes and pools. It also falls from the sky. Now some people are selling it.

In Botswana knowledge of rainwater is deep, long-standing, and metaphysically expansive. Botswana is a place with a long history of political philosophy and debate, a moral imagination expressed in public health practice—whose foundational category is rain.[7] I want to take this imagination and this knowledge seriously as political modality, not in a quest for authenticity, but rather as another source from which alternative possibilities for a planetary politics might be envisioned.[8] Our current moment offers a cautionary tale for those who look to our contemporary forms of governance, markets, or technoscience to apprehend, much less solve, this water crisis.[9] But what other forms of knowledge and governance, ethical platforms, metaphysical possibilities, technological domains are there beyond the limited horizon of state versus market-driven technoscience? Let us look and see what else we might find, how we might reopen our collective imagination to orient ourselves forward.[10]

In this spirit of opening our collective imagination in a moment of such uncertainty that many things must be rethought,

I offer a parable of Tswana rainmaking as a way out of the un-helpful opposition that pits "tradition" versus growth. It is the grounds on which the technology was predicated—the political, metaphysical, and social conditions that enabled rainmaking's efficacy—that hold the moral for this tale. We human beings cannot make rain at present, in Botswana or anywhere else for that matter.[11] The premises of societal and communal life have shifted in ways that do not allow water distribution technolo-gies to operate in a gentle fashion. Where once there was pub-lic healing, in which people attempted to merge rain and social relationships in a dynamic moral economy, now we have public health, in which rain is a necessary calculable element of popu-lation management. Moving out of this technical management mindset is not easy, but let us try.

Rain = happiness

In Setswana the word for happiness is *boitumelo*. It's a collective noun whose root is the verb *go dumela*—to agree, to believe—rendered in the reflexive form, *itumela*. Notice the pairing of agreement and belief, and notice too that *dumela* is the Setswana greeting, the word used to enact the basis of sociality and the ongoing affirmation of personhood. The withholding of greet-ings, to refuse to say dumela to someone is the manifestation of social rupture. You have sat shiva for someone who is now dead to you. It is the opposite of happiness by anyone's accounting. A literal translation of *boitumelo* would be collective self-belief, or collective self-agreement—which locates happiness somewhere firmly in the political.

Historically, symbolically the key process that evidences hap-piness in Setswana is rain, from which flow the good things in life—cattle and children and beer. And the vehicle for ensuring them, the pinnacle of techne—rainmaking. So here we are—rain, cattle, people—a little cluster of joy and well-being, often elusive, difficult to achieve, difficult to maintain.

Water has always been the central substance of political legitimacy in Botswana. It is the precondition of public health and collective well-being, and also the substance from which self-determination flows. *Pula!* (rain) is the national cheer, the name of the currency, and often the name bestowed on a beloved child—Mmapula, Pulane, Pule, Pulafela. Not surprising in an arid land. There are many places where mastery of the desert through water technology mediates political legitimacy: Saudi Arabia, Israel (but not Palestine—where water is withheld), California, to name but a few.[12]

In thinking about water and its distribution and redistribution, we can trace the relationship between collective self-belief and consumptive forms of happiness across shifting technological regimes of governance. I want to do this by considering water technology *as* public health over the *longue durée*. In doing so I suggest that rainmaking in Botswana, as a mode of instantiating collective self-agreement, might offer one way to apprehend (though sadly not to solve) the basic paradox of self-devouring growth that anchors contemporary logics of public health and development.

Rainmaking

A century has passed since the twilight of rainmaking in Botswana. The precise timing of its demise varied across the *various* chiefdoms, and it's a technology that has been revived, either in public or in secret, on numerous occasions. Nonetheless, it has been many, many decades since rainmaking was the central technology by which political legitimacy is evaluated and maintained. At one time, rainmaking was the essential political condition. Consider this praise poem sung for the Bangwaketse chief Segotshane, who ruled for roughly a decade and a half in the mid-nineteenth century:

> If you want a village, first make it rain;
> If you want your juniors . . .
> They have followed the rains;
> People won't come while it is hot . . .
> If you want a village, make it rain;
> If it rains, your people will all come.

society determined by ability to make rain

A village, people, juniors—in other words society itself, and African forms of wealth, the infamous wealth-in-people—are ultimately determined by the ability to make rain.[13]

Much has been written about rainmaking—as public healing, as cosmology, as ritual.[14] I don't want to rehearse those analyses here, meaningful as they are, and much as my description will resonate with and build upon earlier work, especially that of anthropologists of Africa. I am curious about something slightly different—I am interested in the kind of water distribution system on which rainmaking is premised, the kind of water distribution system rainmaking produces, and how that might affect how people approach the technology and its relationship to collective self-agreement and belief. Rain was the basis of self-determination; it enabled women to farm their fields, men to herd their cattle. Rain was socially predicated, and yet rain enabled the individual.

Rainmaking was a technology with a complicated metaphysics. Chiefs, who themselves commanded powerful rainmaking medicines and knowledge, and the professional rainmakers they employed, who did similarly, worked at the interface of an animated ecology that brought frogs, cattle, pangolins, special snakes, clouds, trees, birds, and humans past and present among many entities large and small into a dynamic, metonymic relationship. It required that people work in concert, that they respect the plants and animals and clouds and one another. If rain was property, it belonged to the ancestors not to humans present. Rain was enchanted, sacred, guarded by a magical snake, born of pregnant clouds.

There's no point in romanticizing rainmaking any more than any other political technology. Politics is a nasty business, even Tswana participatory democracy. These were slave-holding societies, which had undertaken their own forms of destructive expansion. As the chiefdoms that would become amalgamated under the ethnonym Tswana migrated into Botswana, they settled and dispersed their cattle in a radius that marked territorial sovereignty. Displaced San people moved into the desert or entered into servitude to the new colonizers. Amid an era of intense political competition on the highveld, one group might plant medicines to disrupt the rain of another so as to secure territory and followers through induced hunger and misery. Rainmaking required that people obey their chief and a host of rules. It required that the chief did likewise. And the historical record shows that this complex technology often failed.

Such failures were politically charged. Collective self-agreement fractured into crosscutting suspicion. When the rain failed, chiefs failed. Women could enter the customary court and physically beat the chief and his advisors. Adolescent boys could sing songs that insulted the chief. When the rain failed, the people also failed. Some were suspected of violating key rules and scorching the earth into heat and dust. Women could be dragged into the court and have their breasts squeezed to see who might have miscarried or left a stillbirth in the veld. Men could be brought similarly if they had slept with an unpurified widow or impregnated a girl who aborted. Those who had would be rubbed clean with *mogaga* bulbs, which cause a raw, itching rash. Or long ago in the nineteenth century they might have been cut on the urethra and their blood mixed with the rain medicines in front of the assembled community. When drought threatened crisis, ritual murder might be a last resort, in order to procure human body parts to strengthen the medicines. The stakes were tremendously high. If the rain failed for too long, famine, and ultimately the breakdown of society itself, could ensue.[15]

Over time collective Christian prayer displaced the pots of medicine as the mode of rainmaking. Here too when the rain failed it was the failure of the people, who were accused of violating the Sabbath or offending God in some other way. And here too the people might rebuke the chief, demanding a return of rainmaking when collective prayer failed.

Over time, rainmaking was supplanted by hydraulic technologies. Nature, in this instance, was no longer an animated ecology to be apprehended and inhabited through metonymic practice, but now an object with limits to be overcome, domesticated, quantified through technology. How did something so fundamental, the substance of life itself, shed the broader dimensions of its power, such that its value was soon reduced to that of economic and public health metrics? And what are the implications of this rationalization of rainwater?

Across the chiefdoms, rainmaking was eventually replaced with prayers and pipes. In Mochudi, the Bakgatla capital, for example, it began in the early 1920s with the regent Isang, whose father, not trusting this ambitious son, had withheld the rainmaking pots, instead entrusting them and the knowledge necessary to use them to Isang's sister, Kgabyana, for safekeeping.[16] He knew water to be a moral substance. Like her father, Kgabyana remained wary of Isang's motives, so she kept the rain medicines hidden. Isang was forced to look elsewhere, even as his people asked him to import a professional rainmaker.

According to Isaac Schapera, Isang "wanted 'something better' for the people. He told them 'how Europeans obtained water,' and pointed out that in western Transvaal, with which many of them were familiar and where part of the tribe still lived, localities previously arid had been made habitable by boring and damming."[17] Of course, people already knew from wells and damming. Botswana is mainly an arid place, with little surface water. Rivers are seasonal, lying there as dry sand during most of the year and then during the rainy season experiencing a brief arterial flow. People dug wells in the sandy bottoms of such riverbeds, and women and girls drew water from these pools for household use, while herd boys brought their cattle to water. But these new wells would be different, the scale larger, the siting better. "He therefore asked that, as he was granting their request for a rainmaker, they in turn should meet his own desire to improve existing water supplies by more scientific methods."[18] He proposed a special tax to be used to hire a water-boring machine. The machine sunk sixteen boreholes, seven of which produced water. But people complained and resented the taxes. They wanted rain.

Let us fast-forward to more recent times. We will see that rainmaking isn't the only complicated water technology that is subject to spectacular failure.

full of rain technology

The Dam

In February 2015, nearly a century after Isang sunk his first bore-holes, the government of Botswana reported that the Gaborone Dam had gone dry. The water level of the central water source for the southeastern region of the country had sunk below 5 percent of capacity, too low to enter the pumps that drive water from the dam into the pipes. The news wasn't surprising, though it was indeed bleak. There was a long run up to this moment: first a serious drought in 2004, a rebound in 2006, then several years later a steady loss of total volume.

modern drought

In August 2012, level 2 water restrictions were imposed, and they remain in effect to this day. These include prohibitions on the watering of gardens, parks, sports fields, and agricultural fields with potable water. Nor was potable water allowed for construction purposes, for use in ornamental fountains, or for spray-washing pavement or vehicles, though buckets could be used to wash cars. "Automatic urinals are prohibited and should all be terminated or retro-fitted within 2 months of the effective date of these restrictions. The filling of all swimming pools with potable water is restricted. Use of potable water by hair salons shall be restricted and closely monitored."

Swimming pools, ornamental fountains, automated urinals, clean automobiles, and new hairstyles at month end—a happiness (and a particular aesthetics of such) now imperiled. Where Gaborone leads, it seems that Los Angeles may well follow.

L.A to follow?

The government Facebook page listing the restrictions also garnered a significant amount of critique in the comments section, from complaints about the ruling party and its alignment with business interests (hotel swimming pools would continue to be filled) to sarcastic jokes about hair salons shampooing customers with dirty water, to remarks about how Botswana would soon become like Zimbabwe—a country whose once admirable urban water infrastructure had eroded, as was evidenced in a series of high-profile cholera outbreaks in 2008–2009.[19]

In January 2013, the secretary of the association of traditional healers accused the president, who is also the paramount chief of the Bangwato, of ignoring his responsibility as rainmaker—

imploring him to return to his home village of Serowe to make rain.[20] By June the government had cautioned that the dam, "the only water oasis for most people in the southern part of the country is slowly drying up." Mr. Selemogwe, the water resources manager of the parastatal Water Utilities Corporation (WUC), announced that the 141.4-million-cubic-meter dam was at 23 percent of capacity. "This amount can only take us less than 10 months, provided people comply with water restrictions and that rationing continues accordingly," he said.[21] In the end the water lasted another nineteen months, nearly double the time predicted, a minor miracle indeed.

In the intervening period, and perhaps accounting for the extra months of water, extraordinary measures were taken. In late August 2013, President Ian Khama publicly urged Batswana to pray for rain in the month of September, the customary month when Batswana begin to turn their attention toward the clouds.[22] The government then organized official prayers.[23] This was not without controversy. The fact of the president of a nominally secular technocratic nation asking citizens to pray was not the problem. Rather, the official organization of prayers provoked predictable power struggles over which churches were invited and how.

Nonetheless, the Water Utilities Corporation "insisted it was urgent that the prayers take place."[24] Throughout the month more prayer meetings would be organized in the hopes of stemming the crisis that the drying of the dam presented. Though by late September, as one commentator noted in the *Sunday Standard* newspaper, "It is still yet to rain as prayers and scientific methods fight for space and recognition amid promising grey skies."[25]

A month or so after the Gaborone Dam went dry, the government completed a massive new dam to the north. But, as of the writing of this book, its pipeline and pumping stations are still under construction and residents of greater Gaborone and the large urban villages that ring it have been warned that water restrictions and regular interruptions in supply will continue for years. Meanwhile, water is being piped in from dams in South Africa via a long-standing agreement, and boreholes continue to pump groundwater.[26] Regular cuts in water supply now join the load-shedding, the rolling blackouts and scheduled power cuts of electricity. In urban neighborhoods of Gaborone and Francistown and in villages and towns across the country, people report lack of water for days and sometimes weeks at a time. In September 2015, water shortages forced PMH, the central referral hospital in Gaborone, to turn patients away, suspend all hemodialysis treatment, and triage gynecology, dental, and pediatrics as patients' relatives arrived bearing bottled water for them.[27]

Amid government complaints that people are wasting water, in a move already undertaken in South Africa, the WUC is installing prepaid water meters, providing a calculated necessary monthly minimum amount per household or community standpipe, beyond which supply will be cut off until residents pay for a further installment. But reading between the lines, it seems that no matter how good the technology, without adequate rain it will be unsustainable over time.

Still need rain ←

In September 2015, Botswana's opposition party, the Umbrella for Democratic Change (UDC), took to the streets in an organized march through Gaborone and neighboring Mogoditshane to protest the crisis of water and electricity. The marchers presented a petition to the Office of the President that began, "We write as messengers of a weary and tearful nation. Our people are thirsty. Our people face the risk of hygiene-related ailments and our entire health care system is at risk. Our businesses are beginning to fold. Foreign investors are reluctant to bet on our country. It is becoming more difficult for our economy to create jobs as many of our youngsters remain jobless."[28]

The ruling party accused the opposition of politicizing the drought.[29] The president's office responded by saying, "We can build dams, drill and equip boreholes, lay pipelines to carry water all over as we have done and continue to do, but if it does not rain, we will always be challenged. The rain is not brought by Government, but Government, if it rains, will harvest and take water to the people."[30]

Put more succinctly, as the president was later quoted, "We are not God and we do not make rain." Such a statement is reasonable, technocratic, pragmatic. But note how the scope of political responsibility has narrowed from the time of rainmaking. Governance is no longer about creating the forms of collective self-agreement necessary to coax the climate, nor about maintenance of the diversity of the animated ecology necessary for rainmaking technology. Its temporal metaphysics are manifest in the five-year plan, not in the recognition that rain condenses past, present, and future in its drops.

The classic folly of development and public health lies in the fantasy by which narrow technological solutions are posed to solve complex political and economic problems. And the classic critique is pointing out the inadequacy of technocratic approaches to what are ultimately problems of maldistribution. But what happens when the technology itself is a redistributive one? What happens if the substance to be redistributed is disappearing—evaporating, at a rapid pace and on a scale that commodification cannot apprehend? In the case of the dam a technocratic approach was used to instantiate and enable a politics of redistribution—much like rainmaking once did. The only problem was that ultimately, the dam too was dependent on the clouds. Calculations were made about evaporation rates, and rainfall levels, and leaking pipes, but there was no mechanism to resacralize the water—no way to say that it is priceless.

In the fall of 2014, I was at a wonderful event at Haverford College where the speakers included Kenyan author Binyavanga Wainana. Referencing the destruction of the Westgate Mall in Nairobi by embarrassed Kenyan authorities in the aftermath of the siege by Al Shabab, Wainana remarked on our strange historical moment. He observed how seemingly fixed pieces of the landscape, including this high-profile mall in Nairobi where a certain kind of happiness was peddled, can suddenly be pierced through and collapsed as though it were merely a cardboard backdrop.

As with Westgate, the 17th Street canal levee of New Orleans, the Fukushima Daichi power plant, or California's vineyards for that matter, the Gaborone Dam was more than it seemed. Not just a water source, it was a key symbolic fixture of a certain kind of postcolonial place, a seemingly natural element of the landscape of a very human-made city. On its (now very dry) shore sits a yacht club particularly popular with whites, and a performance venue. On the road that rings around its southern side fishermen from the abutting low-income neighborhood of Old Naledi used to sell their day's catch or the occasional watermelon. For it to be gone entirely is strange indeed. Though perhaps it is stranger still to lend this kind of permanence to such a manmade structure or to water sources of any sort for that matter, given that Botswana is also home to the Makgadikgadi Pans, a vast ancient sea that dried up millennia ago and across which the president now goes adventuring on his quad bike in his leisure time, in his own personal pursuit of happiness. Nonetheless, the big basin of the now dry dam now sits as a testimony to the impermanence, some would say the folly, of technocratic developmental planning.

The dam on the Notwane River was completed in 1964, on the southern edge of what would become the new capital city of the independent nation of Botswana. This was the heyday of global dam building—an era in which water and land would be taken from some and given to others in the name of growth, in particular feeding the expansion of cities.[31] The World Bank funded Kariba Dam sits on the Zambezi River just to Botswana's northeast. Built only five years earlier to generate electricity for Zambia's copper mines and Zimbabwe's cities, it dwarfed Botswana's small project. Even after the Gaborone Dam's capacity was tripled in the early 1980s, Kariba held more than 1,300 times the volume of water, its construction having displaced tens of thousands of people. Botswana's achievement, by contrast, was modest but nonetheless quite significant.

By 1984, city planners had raised the Gaborone Dam wall by seven meters to accommodate the water needs of the rapidly growing population. Planners in the early 1960s had expected a small city, mainly an administrative center, with some twenty thousand or so residents. At present the greater Gaborone area is home to some twenty-two times that number, while the dam has also served a number of major villages and towns.

The presence of piped water was central to a vision of national development and to a postcolonial public health in Botswana that precious few southern countries have achieved. In the decades after independence, the government of Botswana promised access to clean water to every settlement of five hundred people or more in the form of standpipes. Such a plan embraced a radical vision of public health, the pinnacle of which was encoded in a declaration forged at the World Health Organization (WHO) meeting in Alma-Ata, in the Soviet Republic of Kazakhstan in 1978. This vision, with its emphasis on primary care and community, foregrounded health as a right, whose realization was predicated on state provision of basic infrastructure and goods, thereby providing a platform from which people could break the cycle by which poverty breeds disease, and disease, poverty. In some ways (certainly not all) this was a similar vision to rainmaking, and part of the bedrock of Botswana's miracle.

This is a model of public health on the opposite pole from the depoliticized, technocratic, vertically structured, disease-eradication model that characterized the first twenty years of the health development era, and/or the concentrated investment in costly tertiary care for the few that arose in the wake of the failed disease eradication programs. It is a far cry from the current consumption-based model of public health that is oriented around access to pharmaceuticals, which has been a hallmark of the global health era. It was a moment at odds with self-devouring growth that proved short-lived. The rhetoric of Alma-Ata remained in that emptied-out phrase "health for all in the year 2000"—but the vision was already collapsing, undermined by the oil crisis and the ensuing global recession and debt crisis. The International Monetary Fund (IMF)-led structural adjustment was born as the meeting was winding down. The Bretton Woods economists would be the true arbiters of health and development.

Indeed, public health observers like myself have watched with disdain as clean water and sanitation have been set aside on the multibillion-dollar global health agenda in favor of interventions aligned more and more to pharmaceutical technologies of consumption.[32] The new "LifeStraw" water filtration system, which anthropologist Peter Redfield explains is meant for individual rather than community use, is one such example.[33] This is not to argue against public access to medicines, not in the slightest, but rather to say that access to clean water, safe housing, and adequate nutrition is the basic, empirical bedrock for public health. John Snow's discovery of the relationship between contaminated water and cholera at the Broad Street pump is one of the foundational stories of modern public health. Access to clean water prevents deadly diarrheal disease (a leading killer of children under five), it saves people (mainly women and children) many hours carrying water or queuing for it, and it prevents these same people from contracting waterborne diseases during collection.

When water infrastructure is not maintained, public health erodes—hence the return of the cholera years to Zimbabwe starting in 2008, and the poisonings to Flint, Michigan. So too when water is wholly privatized. In the 1980s, the World Bank began its push for the privatization of water (and many activists pushed back), ironically during the decade the WHO declared as the decade of clean water and sanitation. We've seen in South Africa, in Kwa-Zulu Natal in 2000, how the implementation of water privatization produced 106,000 cases of cholera in a six-month period, resulting in the free basic water policy—the six cubic meters of water per month per family.[34] One could argue, as some economists apparently have, that it is cheaper and makes more sense to provide medicines and oral rehydration salts for diarrheal diseases than to provide potable water for poor people.[35] To think of such economists suffering from relentless diarrhea without access to running water, toilet, or latrine could bring me at least a moment of schadenfreude, of Germanic happiness, I am sure. But let us focus on striving for that Tswana happiness called boitumelo.

According to the logic of public health, the logic of collective bios, the newly independent nation of Botswana did this right. I say this not to celebrate Botswana as some sort of romantic welfare state. Again, politics is a nasty business, and there are plenty of problems—of inefficacy, discrimination, and maldistribution, and increasingly state secrecy and oppression. In 2014, the IMF reported that while Botswana scored well on the human development index, still nearly a fifth of Batswana lived below the poverty line.[36] This is a somewhat arbitrary designation. Many above this magic line are frankly poor. But nonetheless, the broad vision and politics of distribution are worth noting. They made access to water a priority. The water was free for residents (notice not citizens, but residents) who queued at the standpipes. And they paid for it through collective national wealth, mainly in the form of diamonds extracted and marketed through a parastatal, Debswana, and to a much lesser extent through a beef industry fed by boreholes.

Yet it takes a tremendous amount of water, it seems, to run a mine. The diamond mines, like the cattle ranchers, are mining groundwater, a nonrenewable resource, alongside their minerals.[37] There is one ministry for water and minerals. And with mines comes national wealth, and with national wealth also comes private wealth, and with private wealth comes yacht clubs and ornamental fountains and automatic flushing urinals. And with the depletion of water comes privatization and, apparently, prayers.

Listen to the words of Motshwanaesi Thuto, who was interviewed by a journalist for the Pulitzer Center in 2013. Mr. Thuto, in his thirties, is a self-employed resident of Maboane, a small village of two thousand people or so approximately sixty kilometers north of Jwaneng, site of a major Debswana mine and one of the wealthiest towns in the country. Maboane, a poor village, sits in a well field surrounded by over two dozen boreholes that pump water directly to Jwaneng. Its own borehole, however, used to supply water to surrounding villages as well, is often dry or running only at a trickle.

"Yes," Thuto explained, "there is so much suffering and problems here. Is it unfair? We don't see it that way. The diamonds are good for the country. We will do bad so that the country is doing good if that is the way it has to be. If Maboane doesn't have water, we will be thirsty. But if the mines don't have water, how will Botswana live?"[38] Indeed, Botswana's diamonds provide the bulk of the revenue needed to fund the universal health care, the antiretroviral drugs, the tarred roads, and old-age pensions. They are used to pay for eight years of primary education for each child. The diamonds pay for the water system — as much as the reverse.

But not everyone sees the water shortage as a zero-sum game of sacrifice for the national wealth. The comments on the Water Utilities Corporation Facebook page contain myriad complaints by Batswana whose villages and towns have run dry for days at a time. They berate the WUC for their inefficiencies. Many suspect that poorer communities are more likely to be deprived than those where the rich reside. And in June 2015 the Botswana Bureau of Standards finally confirmed what the American embassy had reported three years earlier amid strident denial by the government: much of Botswana's tap water is apparently no longer safe for drinking.[39]

While mining requires a fair amount of water, it is actually agriculture that accounts for the greatest percentage of water use in the country. Though there are several irrigated horticultural schemes (some using treated wastewater), crop production is mainly a rain-fed enterprise. Smallholders rely on rain for their crops of sorghum, maize, millet, and beans. Those with farms smaller than five hectares receive free seed and draft power from the government. Those with farms between five and fifteen hectares receive free seed only, while those with larger holdings receive subsidized seed.

Even with these forms of government assistance, farming is an uncertain practice given the insufficiency and unpredictability of the rain, a situation that is escalating under global climate change. In a context where wage labor opportunities are scarce, farming remains a crucial strategy for Batswana in the rural areas, where women, the poor, disabled persons, and the elderly are concentrated. For rural households, crops in a year with adequate rain provide a substantial portion of the diet. With increasing dependence on food imports, poor households are vulnerable to rising food prices. Geographer William Moseley has described Botswana's development as "growth with hunger."[40]

The water is consumed mainly by the livestock part of the agricultural sector. The Bakgatla may have protested that Isang's boreholes were no substitute for rain, and they have over time been proven right. But by the mid-twentieth century, groups of wealthier, often aristocratic Batswana men began to organize themselves into syndicates. Pooling their resources, they sank boreholes, tapping into underground aquifers in parts of the rangeland that had been previously ungrazed, because of their distance from necessary surface water or wells. This enabled syndicate members to aggregate huge herds, often tended by former serfs/slaves and their descendants, and to command de facto control over large swaths of land that are putatively held in communal tenure—a process that anthropologist Pauline Peters has called "dividing the commons."

Over time even those with smaller herds began to join syndicates, expanding the number of boreholes. Indeed, there are more cattle than people in Botswana, where no less than Lesotho is site of the bovine mystique of which James Ferguson has written.[41] And yet the proportion of households with cattle has fallen from 68 percent in 1981 to 37.5 percent in 2003.[42] While syndicate members, who form a powerful political lobby, pay for the diesel required to pump the water to the surface, the water itself is free. It now seems that it was not only the land that was the commons now divided and essentially all but privatized through a technological scheme, but the water too. It turns out that it is not only ornamental fountains and automated flushing urinals, but also cattle—the ur-category of wealth and redistribution, another formerly sacred substance now called beef— that ultimately requires rain. *Beef requires rain*

But the rains are going away. From 1922 to 1986 the mean annual rainfall in Gaborone was 531 mm, slightly higher than Mochudi, where Isang sunk his boreholes, with 490.9 mm, and Molepolole, with 495.1 mm. The devastating droughts of the 1930s and 1980s are averaged into these figures. Botswana has long had a dry, fickle climate. Yet the pace of drought seems to be increasing. Over the past decade drought has been declared on average once every two years, a doubling of pace from the previous few decades. Climate models predict a decrease of between 50 to 100 mm in annual rainfall averages in southern and southeastern Botswana from 2000 to 2050 (essentially a 10–20 percent

> less rain more evaporation

decline). They also forecast an increase in maximum temperature by 1.5 degrees Celsius or more. Among the models, one predicts an average rise in temperature of more than 3 degrees for 95 percent of the country.[43] In other words, in addition to less rain there will be more evaporation.

And indeed, a massive heat wave accompanied the 2015 drought. In October it reached 42 degrees Celsius (107.6 F) in Botswana's Central district, and by January 2016 there were reports of heat related deaths.[44]

Despite the calls for the Botswana president to return to Serowe and make rain, this is a problem that exceeds even the most efficacious of rainmakers. Rainmaking drew on a regional market in pharmacopeia; it drew rainmakers as public healers from a distance. The animated ecology connected across multiple zones from the ocean to the desert to the highveld. In 1931, when Schapera observed the rainmaker Rapedi making rain, he saw that Rapedi utilized seven different vegetable substances gathered in the bush around Mochudi, each of which had its own metonymic value. In addition he used a variety of animal substances: the feathers, breastbone, and urine of the "lightning" bird (fish eagle), skin from the chest and belly of the crocodile, the body of the *senanatswii* frog, dried belly-skin of a "big sea fish," pieces of the claw of the *kgwadira* bird (bateleur eagle), raw skin from the belly of the hippopotamus, dry dung of the *korwe* bird (red-billed hornbill), a piece of ostrich shinbone with a few pieces of flesh still clinging to it, three scales of the Cape pangolin, whale fat, and the fat of the *phika* snake.[45] The medicines of the past, preserved in fat and ash—the *tshitlho*—were used as the base into which the medicines of the present were then added.

The prayer that Rapedi made while preparing the rain medicine was also regional in its scope. Though he sought to localize rain clouds, to bring rain that goes pitter-pat to Mochudi and the rest of the chiefdom, Rapedi's prayer to animate the medicines marked a genealogy that extended beyond the Bakgatla—drawing together a regional network at once both metaphysical and political. He called on a number of ancestors from the nineteenth century—Sechele, the great Kwena chief, and Gaseitsiwe of the Ngwaketse; he called on Moshoeshoe, the Sotho king and statesman, and Khama, the Ngwato chief and great-great-grandfather of the current president of Botswana. He called on his own ancestors, who Schapera thought were from somewhere on the east coast of South Africa. To them he said, "Refeng pula yalona. Keyalona pula e." (Give us your rain. It is yours, this rain.) Rain could not be commodified, because it already belonged to the past, to the progenitors of today.

But despite the spatial reach of the animated ecology, rainmaking was nonetheless too geographically limited for the clouds of today. Collective self-agreement is hard enough in a chiefdom, a nation-state or region, but it seems to be impossible when the collective is planetary and the demands made on water global in their reach. The mines also consume, in addition to water, vast quantities of fossil fuels and emit their waste, as do the fleet of cars and trucks that private wealth has brought to Batswana. They, along with the diesel borehole pumps on the cattle ranches, and the perpetually troubled and often dysfunctional new Morupule B power plant—the coal-fired power station in Palapye built by Chinese contractors and intended to produce 80 percent of the energy needs for the nation—these technologies are actually technobiologies.[46] They are changing the clouds and even the sun itself; they are altering biology on a vast scale.

Botswana has a national climate change policy, which includes plans for a solar-generated power plant and a range of other new technologies that are intended to green the nation. And yet such local and regional political technologies are insufficient to make rain at home. Morupule B and Debswana are but small instantiations of a vast network of self-devouring growth—refineries from Houston to Abadan, factories from Beijing to Moscow, automobiles from Chile to Italy, the jet planes in which I fly to Botswana and in which I return home. Botswana ratified the United Nations Framework Convention on Climate Change in 1994 and has been a signatory to related international instruments, but it does not have the power to influence and achieve collective self-agreement.

Of course, it would be disingenuous to detach Botswana from China's factories or Saudi Arabia's oil refineries, because with collective wealth has come escalating consumption. If rain and cattle and people still bring boitumelo, they are joined by new cars, Kentucky Fried Chicken, clothing, hairdos, washing machines, and cell phones. All of this self-devouring growth is connected in an economy of happiness even more far-flung than Rapedi's pharmacopeia.

In other words, rain today is not the rain possessed by Moshoeshoe and his contemporaries. It belongs to a more recent generation of humans past, ancestors from the time of self-devouring growth—a time of increasingly scarce and dirty water. It is not only man-made water sources like the Gaborone Dam that are drying up. To take a particularly egregious example, think of the Aral Sea, which straddles Uzbekistan and Kazakhstan (though far from Alma-Ata). Once the fourth largest lake in the world, its shores lined with fishing ports and seaside resorts, it is now a mainly a toxic sand desert. The Aral Sea was central to Soviet development schemes, which used the rivers that fed it to irrigate vast areas of the steppe for cotton farming and urban development. Over time, ever-larger quantities of chemicals were required to produce a crop as the quality of soil and water declined.

This continued in the post-Soviet era of economic liberalization, which did away with collective farms and social safety nets, replacing them with land rental schemes and cotton quotas. At present 92 percent of the 53 billion cubic meters of water consumed each year in Uzbekistan goes to agriculture, the vast majority of it absorbed into the cotton sector. Eventually this self-devouring growth killed the sea and its tributaries, leaving behind a toxic wasteland, producing thousands of tons of dust made of pesticides and fertilizers and chemicals. Predictably, high rates of cancer, birth defects, and a range of other afflictions have made the former Aral Sea basin one of the unhealthiest places in the world. But this toxic dust exceeds the region — it has been carried by the wind as far away as Greenland and Japan.[47] The rain, the cotton that I and many of you readers may be wearing, the failed utopianisms of economies past, as much as the cynical kleptocracies of economies present, are part of a planetary ecology. Though we've experimented with rendering rain as private property from Bolivia to Colorado, we cannot find a way to make sense of our current ownership over the clouds of the future — to know ourselves as ancestors, antecedents of the rainmakers of a later age.

Resurrection

More than a year after its death, the Gaborone Dam was resurrected. In March 2016, after so many years of drought, unexpected rains arriving too late for the plowing season brought flooding to large villages within the catchment area of the dam, yet the drought persisted.[48] But by August of that year Radithupa Radithupa, Botswana's chief meteorologist, told the waiting public that the El Niño cycle was drawing to a close and giving way to La Niña. Though many dared not hope, he predicted ample rains in the growing season to come.

In November Radithupa Radithupa instructed reluctant farmers to ready their plows.[49] The sky broke open and everyone drank in the sublime scent of the newly soaked ground. By January the rains were so heavy and insistent that the Hatsalatladi Bridge in the large village of Moshupa collapsed. Days later the Mosope Bridge on the A10 road washed away. Some lost their homes and property in the floods. Others filled their cisterns from the sky as the village taps in Moshupa suffered continued water shortages from burst pipes.[50] By late January water was pouring into the Gaborone Dam from its tributaries, and at month's end it was over 30 percent full.[51] *Pula!*

Within weeks Cyclone Dineo arrived from Mozambique with strong winds, lightning, and torrential rain. The ensuing floods caused closure of the busiest segments of the A1 highway, those connecting Lobatse–Gaborone and Kanye–Lobatse. Other roads were also washed away, bridges destroyed, and motorists stranded.[52] Parts of the railway line were washed out and a train derailed at Lobatse, flipping on its side. Schools were closed, homes were lost, and the displaced were given tents, food baskets, blankets, and other supplies.[53] The Botswana Defense Force was called in to assist with the emergency.

The Bamalete Lutheran Hospital in Ramotswa was hard

hit. Doctors were trapped in their homes by the floodwaters. Corpses had to be moved from the hospital morgue to a funeral home in town, and many patients were transferred to Princess Marina Hospital, forty kilometers away in Gaborone. Suddenly the Gaborone Dam was full to capacity, as residents of nearby Tlokweng eyed its spillway nervously, fearing the necessary evacuation if it overflowed its banks.[54] More floods came, but they were to the north in Nata and Gweta, on the shores of the salt pans, where roads were rendered impassable and a child suffering a severe malaria attack had to be airlifted over flooded roads by helicopter to a nearby hospital. More homes were lost, the mud-brick houses of the rural poor were the most vulnerable to collapse under heavy rain.[55]

Rainmakers of old like Rapedi sought soft, extended rain. Such rain was celebrated in song as rain that went "pitter pat." Strong storms could destroy. Lightning was a sign of malfeasance, of envy. La Niña was neither soft nor gentle, but after so many years of thirst, her arrival was hailed as a miracle. On 5 March, with the storms now over, President Khama and his cabinet gathered on the shore of the Gaborone Dam and led the nation in prayer, declaring a national day of Thanksgiving.[56]

La Niña brought persistent drenching rain and flooding to parched California as well, another place where the paradoxes of growth and consumption have eviscerated much and where the drought had been long and brutal. The false prophets of fecundity in the Central Valley, in the form of vast quantities of almonds and pomegranates, long ago drowned the voices of any ancestors who might enforce a collective moral imagination of distribution. The hoarding of water and use of chemical pesticides in the name of growth had long become normalized. The longed-for rains turned violent. Landslides destroyed Highway 1 in and out of Big Sur, turning it for one long summer into a tourist-free paradise. Landslides also blocked sections of Highway 17 in the Santa Cruz Mountains south of Silicon Valley. By spring the desert bloomed in untold magnificence and the rebirth of new green growth appeared across the region. Months later and parched again, the now dry remnants of that brief fecundity ignited into flame and smoke.

So what are we to make of this — this shift from rainmaking to hydrology — from public healing to public health? If rainmaking was a leveling technology, one that was predicated on collective, coordinated engagement, and then delivered the goods (water) in a widely dispersed form, the developmental state has carried some part of this ethos forward through redistributive schemes that have steadily decreased the vulnerability of Batswana living in poverty. This is a good thing. Yet at the same time, the gap between rich and poor has continued to grow. If there is now a minimum under which the developmentalist state seeks not to let people fall, there is no maximum to which they might strive.

And what are we to make of this slowly unfolding crisis of thirst? Though reuse of treated wastewater promises a potential short-term technological amelioration of the drying of the land, if the rains continue to fail at an accelerating pace, just as the diamonds are depleted, perhaps descendants of the former slaves, the autochthonous bushmen, the original residents, will have bided their time long enough to inherit the thirstland again.

Rainmaking necessitated an ecological mode, a set of elements that drew the world together into a microcosm — and a mode of political agreement that accepted hierarchy, but also expressed the dynamic tensions that sustained it. It took a moral-enough world for government to work and that was an accepted metaphysical fact. What is the difference between public healing in an animated ecology, where the past is always present, and public health as a technoscientific problem to be solved in an ever future-oriented telos? In an animated ecology water has value in how it condenses (literally) the success or failure of moral relationships, of political vision, of collective self-agreement, however hierarchical the collective. These are relationships that supersede the human, given their interspeciated and sacred aspects. Water is held by the ancestors — it is "theirs." But it isn't private property and it cannot be bought and sold, only requested by those who must demonstrate their worthiness to receive this gift. In development and public health, water is also an index of political efficacy rendered, a resource that is either under- or overvalued in calibration to its supply, or a basic human right — a liberal formulation that ultimately derives from a private property model that privileges human beings as individuals only by way of their claims to citizenship/membership in a political entity and cleaves them off from other species.

The animated ecology is not a nature out there upon which humans act or from which humans extract. It is a living manifestation of a tangle of historical relationships between entities large and small, humans past and present. In an animated ecology, I would suggest, limits on growth are always present in some form. But in a developmental state where nature—now separated from humans—becomes an object with limits to be overcome, domesticated, quantified through technology, endless growth is the very point. The developmentalist state is not the only political formation with this relationship to growth. It seems foundational to liberalism, hence Malthus; to empire, hence the Soviet cotton schemes; and of course to capitalism. Within this telos of growth, what kind of bios is possible? What sort of technopolitics can we imagine will lead to what sort of happiness? What political form can again take hold of the clouds, the rain, the sun?

2

In the Time of Beef

FOR MUCH OF THE TWENTIETH century the people of southern Africa were hungry. Seasonal hunger had long been familiar, as had the periodic famine. But the demands of European colonialism, with its insatiable thirst for labor and resources, combined with the environmental vagaries of the region to intensify the gnawing many felt in their bellies. Bechuanaland was no different. In the 1930s, amid drought and worldwide economic depression, people fashioned special girdles to wear around their waists to contain their hunger in the absence of food. In the 1950s and 1960s malnutrition dominated public health concerns, amplifying and combining with infectious disease to threaten infants and young children in particular. Fast-forward a half century and while many people in Botswana still know hunger, they are supported by a welfare system based on claims to the distribution of collective wealth in the form of diamonds, which provides a cushion against malnutrition and outright starvation. This is a good thing. Meanwhile, many others in Botswana are now contending with overconsumption. Obesity, hypertension, and diabetes have replaced malnutrition as principal public health concerns. Beef consumption is but one element in this changing body. But it is a significant one, not only in terms of diet but also as a synecdoche of the paradox of self-devouring growth.

The British drew their protectorate, Bechuanaland, into the beef market in the 1950s when the British themselves were still hungry from the war. At independence Botswana's abattoir was reportedly the largest and most technologically sophisticated in the southern hemisphere. Over time, their preferential access to the European market has more or less held through a series of international negotiations. This access has helped to maintain Botswana's position as Africa's largest beef exporter, a small but vital contributor to the multibillion-dollar global beef industry, in which some 59 million metric tons of beef were produced in 2016 from the growth and slaughter of cattle.

The shift from cattle to beef is one of disenchantment, of the commodification of sentient beings, and also one of emergent ecological crisis. As we learned in the preceding parable, beginning in the 1930s wealthier cattle owners organized themselves into corporate syndicates and sunk a series of boreholes in the veld in Botswana. Rather than fencing and enclosing the commons as had happened in England, in Botswana those with boreholes commanded large areas of the communal rangeland that otherwise cattle could not graze for lack of water.[1] Over time, the number of boreholes expanded, as did the cattle population. Eventually the rate of water consumption by cattle began a process of mining the groundwater—drinking down the water table faster than the underground aquifers can recharge, even as warming temperatures and drought are increasing the pace of evaporation. In other words, an abundance of food is contributing to a shortage of water. This is but one example of self-devouring growth; if you read on, you will find others.

Botswana is a place where individualism and communalism have long been held in dynamic tension, where hierarchy unfolds through a moral imagination whose central object of desire is bovine.[2] In Botswana appreciation of cattle is aesthetically deep and metaphysically potent. Cattle have been the subject of poetry, prayer, and reverie and the symbolic hub of ritual and meaning. They have long been the mode of wealth in the most expansive sense of the term. Beginning gradually in the mid-twentieth century, however, cattle have been rendered as beef—a techno-economic object. In the process the aesthetic imagination has been reoriented around the taste of grilled steak, canned corned beef, the wedding and funeral staples of pounded beef (*seswaa*), as well as the money to be earned from the sale of animal parts in the global beef market.

Batswana are sophisticated techno-scientific players in a global market, and this parable is not a straightforward tale of nostalgia for a lost pastoral past of cows swishing their tales in the veld while noble herdsmen look on. How could it be? Over the same time period there has been a shift from recurrent hunger to abundant food. In the past, cattle were a mode of subjugation by which seniors managed juniors and men maintained power over women. Where once only men could truly possess these animals, now women too can own and manage herds. Where once cattle were the objects of envy that propelled violence in the form of cattle raiding, war, and witchcraft, now beef is actively distributed globally, and domestically it has become the substance of festivals rife with music and celebration; in a regime of high unemployment it is an economic lifeline—forming the basis for women's vending to urban workers on their lunch break. Development has its paradoxes, but its benefits cannot easily be ignored. Instead, as we follow the hermeneutics of the cow, the nostalgia you feel here is for a time when "progress" felt less like immanent collapse, when future health seemed like a definable goal; for a time when the distributary mechanism of the cow, while certainly not even, was at least more equitable than the techno-capitalist present; for a time when humans thanked animals for the gift of their flesh.

Desiring Cattle

Batswana, like many other people in southern Africa, have long been passionate about cattle. The following two poems, published in the early 1940s in the journal *Bantu Studies* and deploying imagery common to a long-standing genre of Tswana poetry, suggest the nature of desire.[3]

> 1
> Stout-one of arms (weapons)
> Preparer of liquid food.
> God with the long, straight nose,

When it lows, saying "moo,"
Women say "it says, 'moo,'"
Men say, "it's saying '[to] arms again!'"
Ah! Animal of my father—red female.
God with the moist nose.
A short sip of something hot.
[This] god has eaten my father,
And as for me, he'll eat me too.
Animal with the moist nose.

2

A heavy wooden bowl of my father
When I have eaten from it, my heart is glad
For it's the bowl of my parents
Wooden bowl for sweet gravy of the cow
Lovely cattle of our home
One alone, is sweetness
Missing one, alone, is sorrow
Dark blue-grey cow—one who robs of sleep
Cow with the many spots
One with the melodious tongue
Stout-one of weapons
Preparer of liquid food
God, with the moist nose.

As the anthropologist Hoyt Alverson observed in his analysis of
these poems, "The cow here is not a salable commodity, an item
of exchange. It is the object of ecstasy."[4] But what does it mean to
find ecstasy in another being, another species? What did it mean
for the cow herself to be the subject of such reverie? What kind
of passion was this? In the nineteenth century and for much of
the twentieth it seems this was a passion to possess the world.
People, food, status, beauty—the power inherent in all of this
was held in the microcosm of the cow. This cow—stout one of
weapons—was worth fighting and perhaps dying for. This cow
held the world together. Her voice lowed the music of life itself.
Her dark blue-gray coat was the color of a rain cloud. In her flesh
lay a metaphysical potency unlocked during ritual sacrifice and
medical practice. In her body lay a map of the family and the

reach of the sovereign. In her milk—sweet gravy, liquid food—lay the taste of fertility, and it was delicious.

Jean and John Comaroff, invoking Mauss, explain that once cattle were "total social phenomena"—that is, things that contained "all threads of which the social fabric is woven."[5] Who would have thought that this object of desire, the Tswana total social fact, could someday wind up in the microwaves of pubs across England or doled out in school lunchrooms in Norway? How on earth was this improbable development achieved, and what does it mean for the bovine-human interspeciated system of health and well-being? What kind of total social fact is the cow now?

Total Social Fact

In the nineteenth century and for much of the twentieth cattle were at the center of Tswana life. Milk—liquid food, sweet gravy—was collected in skin bags and allowed to curdle into the staple *madila*. Beef was eaten (only) at ritual occasions and festivities, divided into gifts and tribute, and dried into *biltong* for storage. At the end of the agricultural season, with the harvest complete, cattle browsed on the stalks of millet and sorghum and pumpkin and beans, clearing fields and fertilizing them with their dung. Women used dung to smear the walls of their houses, insulating them from the heat and cold, and retarding insects. Dung was also burned for cooking. Children were carried nestled in slings made from hides on the backs of their mothers, aunts, and sisters. Hides were also worked into leather aprons and the thong used to make the mesh of men's folding chairs. By the late nineteenth century, with the introduction and widespread adoption of the plow and oxcart, oxen were used for draught power and transporting loads.

Cattle created the connective tissue that held the social world together and enabled its reproduction. The exchange of cattle was fundamental to the process of marriage, and connected "cattle-linked" siblings as animals received in the marriage of a sister could in turn be used to foster the marriage of her brother. Cattle given in tribute by the people to the chief,

massCattle could be sold for $

and those loaned by the chief to the people, manifested sovereignty in bovine form. Cattle lent out to be herded in networks of exchange and patronage deposited the gerontocratic and class-based hierarchies of Tswana communities in milk pails of "sweet gravy." Boys, young men, and lower-status men — including *batlhanka* (serfs/slaves) herded the cattle of their seniors, consuming their milk and madila. Cattle in a father's herd could be already promised to sons and daughters.

This was a mode of property at once collective and individual. At the moment of its death, the animal revealed itself to be a microcosm of family and community, mapped through the variety of tastes and textures of beef contained within a single beast. Listen to anthropologist Isaac Schapera's description of the partible animal:

> Meat obtained from the slaughter of any domestic animal is shared by all the members of the household. Special portions are allotted to the wives, elder sons, and elder daughters. Some of it must also be given to such near relatives as paternal and maternal uncles and aunts, well-defined rules laying down which particular portions must be given to each category of relative. Thus, among the Kgatla, a man whenever he slaughters an ox or a goat should give the head (*tlhogo*) to his maternal uncle; the forelegs (*letsogo*) to his senior paternal uncles, his elder brothers, or his eldest son; the hindquarters (*serope*) to his junior paternal uncles; the flanks (*motlhana*) to his paternal aunts or daughters; the backbone (*mokoto*) and intestines (*mala*) to his father or junior paternal uncles; the liver (*sebete*) to his wife and younger children; the spleen (*lebete*) and perhaps a hindquarter (*serope*) to his herdboys; and the entrails (stomach, lungs, and heart) to the men at his *kgotla*. The chest (*sehuba*) and belly (*mpa*) he keeps for himself and his family, while the ribs (*dithupa*) he may give to any friend or person he likes or keep for himself. He may also, if he feels like it, present his headman with the *sehuba* or with a *letsogo*.[6]

Like human beings, each cow, bull, or ox had its own unique qualities marked in poetry through reference to the beauty of coloration. Even well into the 1970s Alverson "heard Tswana sit and talk about the nuances in the physical appearance, behavior, or history of a single cow for an hour."[7] And like human beings, these unique qualities existed in tension with a socially consti- tuted existence, such that cattle were imbued with the essence of their owners and served as proxies for them to some extent. This very quality of cattle made them potent agents, through which people sought to transform the world in ritual and medicine.[8] Adolescent boys awaiting initiation dressed as cattle to signify their liminal status and demand to be made men. For Batswana the nature/society binary was not an ontological assumption but rather an avid process that they undertook with purpose. Human exceptionalism was made possible through the careful manipulation of an animated ecology in which cattle occupied the threshold between metaphysical registers. People prayed for cattle and they prayed with cattle. They doctored their cattle to keep them strong and safe, and they used cattle to doctor their people, their society.

But the apotheosis of the cow, the bull, the ox, was not in opposition to their material qualities and value; rather, they were merged. As anthropologist Jacqueline Solway explains,

> To look at one's cattle, one takes stock. One takes stock of
> their aesthetic value, their beauty and dignity; one takes
> stock of their number; but one also takes stock of one's life
> as reflected in one's herd. One notes the ox that is a descen-
> dant of the cow purchased after the second mine contract, the
> cow from a sister's bridewealth, the cow from one's mother's
> brother and the bull from a sister's child and so on. As such
> they are embodiments — living icons — of particular social and
> spiritual relationships, as well as of general cultural values, and
> their presence alone evokes strong cultural sentiments and a
> sense of well-being. I was often told of how nice it was "just
> to look at one's cattle." . . . Cattle link the economic spheres of
> production, exchange and consumption and they are a link par
> excellence between the world of objects and that of meaning.[9]

Meanings, of course, are subject to change, and so too are objects—especially biological ones, like cows and bulls and oxen. Today's cattle are not the same as those of a century ago. Commodification is a technobiological process. The substance of the organism itself is changed. Cattle are bred, fed, watered, doctored, and indeed killed differently than long ago. The growth of the cow and the entire national herd has accelerated. So too has the human population who consumes the cow. How was this accomplished? And what did it mean? Commodification is also a metaphysical process, as we know from Marx, one that is totally disconnected from living beings and the relationships that define their existence. Nature and society were being conceptualized and separated in new ways in the interest of growth. Indeed, cattle were at one time recognized to be both subjects and objects. The man who pierced the arteries at the throat of the animal to bring about its death first spoke with the animal gently, and with gratitude. Today, bovine subjectivity remains in the small herds that some families keep, but for those cattle held in larger herds it is actively erased.

In the nineteenth century British liberals waxed optimistic about the possibilities of free trade for southern African redemption. They claimed that capitalism, private property, and commerce had the power to liberate Africans—to free them from the fetish of the cow and (ironically enough) the darkness of human oppression and slavery. But in arid Bechuanaland there were only two things for selling in the colonial market beyond the occasional surplus of grain—cattle and human labor. And as we've already seen, cattle and humans were conjoined, were interspeciated familiars. So what might it mean to find your supposed freedom in the sale of yourself, of your total social fact? And how on earth was this accomplished?

British colonial rule beginning in the late nineteenth century put an end to wars over cattle and marked the precipitous decline of cattle raiding. Yet violence persisted, displaced into new forms. Colonialism also forced men to sell animals and to send their sons out to work in the newly opened South African mines in order to pay the taxes the British demanded. It trapped women behind in Bechuanaland, beholden to male relatives whose oxen plowed the fields women farmed. Until the late nineteenth century there was little commercial opportunity to purchase or sell cattle. But with the new migrant labor economy brought by the South African mineral revolution, new pathways to possession emerged.

The opening of an import/export market in cattle was only the first step in the move from cattle to beef, from occasional, reluctant slaughter to a system of boreholes, fences, feedlots, vaccinations, and certifications whose endpoint was the death of the cow and the sale and consumption of beef. By 1946 the census revealed a cattle population of some 628,800 — about twice the number of humans.[10] These proportions have persisted, with humans and cattle both growing in tandem, amid devastating setbacks — famines, epidemics, epizootics.

Until the 1950s Bechuanaland lacked a domestic market for beef. One could not walk to the corner and buy a kilo of mince any more than one could procure a kilo of tofu. Groups of men would slaughter an animal for a sacrifice, wedding, or funeral; the country lacked a slaughterhouse. Cattle for sale were exported on the hoof to South Africa. This began as more than a trickle. In 1911–1912 already some 14,000 head of cattle were sold through the border town of Lobatse. By 1953 the figure was 71,116 and an additional 7,500 animals slaughtered for domestic consumption in Lobatse's newly opened abattoir. The construction of the slaughterhouse was prompted by a new colonial development scheme focusing on beef, and the opening of a British beef market, which was hungry for imports after the contraction of supply from the United States. By the late 1950s, with British encouragement, beef exports in Bechuanaland had surpassed those of live cattle.[11]

But it took many decades for the commodification of cattle to begin to reconfigure their value away from ecstasy and toward capitalist investment. Alverson describes the process as he found it in the early 1970s as a generational one: "The young differ from

no longer ecstasy

the elders in seeing cattle both as something beautiful and as capital investment, which to be used effectively must be sold when the animals fetch their best market price. Elders sell cattle in moments of desperation; to sell at all means that to some extent one has failed. When they do sell, they choose the oldest, scrawniest, and most diseased of their beasts, which usually nets them very little cash."[12]

The year of independence—1966—was a banner one for beef, with approximately 165,000 cattle sold for slaughter or exported on the hoof. Such high numbers sound promising. Many of the men were white ranchers for whom cattle had never been interspeciated familiars. And yet to the Batswana men whose cattle found their way to market, not to mention for the animals themselves, this was instead a sign of tragedy—sale as failure, rather than as success. Despite the spread of boreholes, the massive drought between 1965 and 1969 was deadly for cattle. In a drought, cattle starve, even if they are regularly watered. Without rain, there was not enough food for them to graze. Some owners held out, others availed themselves of the market. Alverson explained, "In market terms, this represented for many individuals an 'economic' loss of about 90 to 95 percent of their worth. Still, this kind of calculation is meaningless to the [older] Tswana, who view the loss of cattle much as we would the loss of a great objet d'art—that is to say, as incalculable."[13] But by this time such sentiments toward cattle had begun to shift among younger Batswana.

For the newly independent nation the cattle industry was an obvious choice around which to focus its development efforts. Who could have known that vast deposits of diamonds would be discovered and developed in the coming years and that eventually the diamonds would subsidize the growth of the cow?[14] Cattle were already a form of investment, already a market, already of great interest to the elite. At the time Seretse Khama, president of the new nation, owned the largest herd in the country, with some 18,000 head.[15] The cattlemen also included the white ranchers in the country, who despite their small numbers wielded disproportionate political and economic influence and commanded large herds.[16] Boreholes to provide water points on the veld, and other "improved" veterinary methods, had increased inequality in cattle ownership, and independence saw a range of policies that prompted the further consolidation of the professional pastoralist—the cattleman, the rancher.[17]

The establishment of the parastatal Botswana Meat Commission (BMC) in 1967 marked the developmental rise of this new mode of interspeciation, this new mode of desire. If cattle were individual living beings, beef was a substance that required standardization. Solway, in telling the biography of one such cattleman in Kgalagadi, notes that in 1967 he switched from agro-pastoralism to focus his attention on capitalist cattle rearing and the emerging beef industry. In that same year this rising cattleman ceased giving his animals names. Needless to say, the slaughter of a named being is quite different than that of an unnamed unit of value.

At its founding in 1967 the BMC took over the abattoir at Lobatse, and over the next few decades it would construct two more slaughterhouses. Eventually, in 2006, the BMC began to promote a system of feedlots for "finishing" the growth of beef. Feedlots had existed previously but in 2001 were used for only 3 percent of cattle. As a team of consultants from the Food and Agriculture Organization of the United Nations (UN FAO) and Botswana's Ministry of Agriculture advocated in 2013, "Feedlotting increases weight, but also improves carcass conformation, grading and fat cover, leading to a higher price per kilogram and more kilograms per carcass."[18] The conversion of cattle to beef at slaughter now complete, humans who once gazed at the beauty of animals, delighting in their voices and graceful movements, have turned their eye toward the quality of "carcass conformation, grading and fat cover." One might add that feedlotting requires huge quantities of grain. Somewhere else in the world maize and perhaps soybeans, awash in agrochemicals, must be grown not for hungry humans, but for Botswana's feedlots.[19]

By 2011 an American veterinarian working as a consultant in Botswana would describe the system as follows. Though things rarely worked this efficiently in practice, and the BMC is no longer the one to oversee the feedlots, it nonetheless gives a sense of the scheme as designed:

> The cattle are bought by the BMC at the farm and then moved from the farm to the hired feedlots for fattening and disease monitoring before they are slaughtered at the BMC abattoir and the meat is shipped off to Europe. For every movement of animals across zone borders, the vets from the government Department of Veterinary Sciences need to be there filling out a permit for each animal detailing which animal was on which truck, moved to which pen in the feedlot on whatever day, and linked to an account containing all vaccinations, medications, disease status, everything you would ever want to know about that particular animal. This may seem an overly intricate attention to detail, but this traceability is crucial to any food production system. Suppose there is an outbreak of disease, thirty people in Norway get sick from eating beef. We need to be able to go back and see where exactly in the system the problem happened so we can prevent it from happening again. Were all of the cases from the same farm? The cattle whose meat was eaten, were they all loaded onto the same truck and caught a disease in transit? Maybe they were living in the same pen in the feedlot where a broken pipe has leaked water contaminated with pathogens that needs fixing. Any link in the chain can be weak, *and each sirloin eaten has its own chain that we need to be able to follow straight back to the day it was born.* The feedlots and the BMC have spent millions of Pula in the past few months to update their facilities to reach EU compliance. New sick pens have been built for animal isolation, new color-coded rows have been implemented to coordinate ear tags with cattle placement, a universal electronic cataloguing system has been implemented for the feedlots and BMC so that everyone is working on the same page in the same way.[20] (emphasis mine)

Cattle are now raised in Botswana in the hopes they will be eaten as beef in Europe, where their flesh will fetch the best price. The slippages between beef and cattle are global and institutionalized such that each and every "sirloin" has a birthday. Where once the birthday of the cow or ox or bull was indeed a moment to be remembered, a form of interspeciated kinship that intersected with and crisscrossed human kinship, this sirloin birth marks a new cosmology, a new metaphysics of the animal stripped down to its biological essence. Throughout this process, however, the herds held by some families have remained as repositories of the imagination.[21] These repositories are further renewed by some urbanites who purchase cattle to start herds as a mark of their adulthood.[22] The cattle post, the ultimate site of rest and pleasure in Botswana, is also a portal into an older mode of interspeciation and sociality.

Sickness and Mass Slaughter

In the late 1970s the Ministry of Agriculture would support the construction of the parastatal Botswana Vaccine Institute (BVI), which would go on to partner with Merial (the animal health division of Sanofi pharmaceuticals) to research and manufacture vaccines for livestock.[23] A veterinary service would further support the work of the BVI and the BMC. The Department of Veterinary Service would also oversee the construction of a network of over five thousand kilometers of cordon fences to segment the country into livestock zones in the hopes of containing disease outbreaks. As this elaborate system of hygiene suggests, cattle, like all living beings, are vulnerable. This vulnerability is persistent and is enmeshed with the vulnerability of humans, as Batswana have long known. Working against the fantasy of technobiological manipulations, vulnerability merely shifts shape and form.

In February 1995, as cross-border movements increased along the once militarized divide between Botswana and a now postapartheid Namibia, a pressing security threat emerged in Botswana's northwestern Ngamiland region. Contagious bovine pleuropneumonia appeared in the Ngamiland cattle herd, apparently imported from an outbreak in neighboring Namibia. By April 1996 the Botswana government's Department of Animal Health and Production had ordered the culling of the entire

Ngamiland herd of some 320,000 cattle. This move succeeded in halting the epizootic at the fence separating that livestock zone from the rest of Botswana, though it could not replenish the aquifer consumed by now-tainted beef. Over time, government programs compensated farmers for lost herds and the district was restocked. But by that time many farmers had experienced irreparable economic collapse and left cattle keeping altogether, further concentrating the national herd in the hands of the wealthy. And lest we forget, a third of a million docile, large, nonpredatory mammals had been killed in some form of mass economic prophylaxis.

This was not the first time that an epizootic had threatened herds in the region and helped further ongoing processes of economic restructuring. Nor was it the first time that killing was repurposed as a health intervention. A century earlier the rinderpest epizootic devastated much of the African continent from the Red Sea all the way to the Cape of Good Hope. It took only twenty-five days for the virus to move across Bechuanaland, decimating herds in its wake. According to historian Pule Phoofolo, "[Among the Bangwato] by mid-1894 it was estimated that only two or three head of cattle remained alive for every hundred that had existed at the beginning of the year. . . . At the end of July 1894 the London Missionary Society representative, H. Williams, estimated that only seventy herds had been spared from the ten thousand held by Chief Sebele."[24] Overnight the staple food of soured milk (madila) disappeared.

Meanwhile, the colonial veterinary service, facing a novel disease, ordered the slaughter of infected cattle and those they suspected as infected. This did not help matters, as Pule explains: "Even more explosive, certainly, were the political undertones of these anti-rinderpest measures. Slaughtering cattle was a certain invitation to trouble, especially when the shooting was done by the very people cattle-owners suspected of introducing the plague. 'They tell me you are a doctor,' quipped one of the Tswana chiefs defiantly in conversation with a white veterinarian who was advising the slaughter of his people's infected cattle, 'but can you do nothing but kill?'"[25] As with the 1995 cattle pneumonia, this earlier immense loss of animals drove southern African *culling?*

men into the wage-labor economy, a fact the London Missionary Society cheered. African hunger and poverty proved a boon to the new labor-hungry goldmines of the Witwatersrand, who promptly slashed their wages by 30 percent. By the time wages were converted back into herds, the twin yokes of racial capitalism and colonialism had tightened.

This was not the first mass culling. In 1858–59 the Xhosa people on the southeastern coast of Africa, in the face of brutal colonial violence and encroachment, responded to a prophecy by slaughtering hundreds of thousands of cattle whose meat they would not consume in an effort to bring about a new world. This millennial movement that sought purification through slaughter divided the polity and ultimately failed, bringing the Xhosa firmly under the racist, colonial thumb of the Cape.[26]

Nor would the Ngamiland culling be Botswana's last. In 2011 the government ordered the slaughter and subsequent burning of some ten thousand animals in veterinary zones 6 and 7 — this time on the border with Zimbabwe.[27] Despite the elaborate system of fences, certifications, and the buffer zone of vaccinated cattle on the northeastern border, the highly contagious foot-and-mouth disease (FMD) had crossed into Botswana. Though not in itself particularly deadly, FMD can produce lameness and wasting, and significantly, it renders beef ineligible for sale to any foot-and-mouth-free country. Though the government maintains a cordon fence at the border, some suspected that illegal sales of animal products from Zimbabwe were to blame.[28] Farmers in the area, including cattle-owning members of parliament, chiefs, and councilors, were furious at the culling decision. Meeting with the minister of agriculture, they blamed government incompetence for the entry of disease into the country, protested the forced slaughter, and complained that government compensation inevitably amounted to less than the market value of their cattle. Xenophobia toward Zimbabweans was extended to their bovine familiars. Yet despite impassioned declarations of refusal by many at the meeting, eventually some ten thousand animals, some of them "rare and expensive breeds," were put to death.[29]

The 2011 FMD outbreak, which in addition to zones 6 and 7

also occurred in Ngamiland, couldn't have come at a worse time for Botswana's beef industry. The year had started well, with the parastatal BMC confident after a year of record slaughter and sale of 179,000 animals in 2010, nearly a third more than the previous year. This brought the slaughter closer to the target capacity of a quarter million cattle per annum, around which the industry was organized. The CEO of the Botswana Meat Commission, David Falepau, credited the new Direct Cattle Purchase Scheme with the rising sales figures. Under this program the BMC created incentives for owners to sell young cattle to be fattened on feedlots before slaughter. Falepau explained, "Rather than farmers rearing them for five years, we decided, through the DCP, to purchase the animals at weights too light for slaughter and feedlot them. . . . We are trying to purchase more calves and less older cattle. . . . In developed countries [like the desirable EU market], they wean animals at 250 kilogrammes, then put them on farms to feed on grass to 380 kilogrammes, then feedlot to 420 kilogrammes."[30]

And yet by the time of the culling, the EU had already temporarily banned Botswana beef from their market. This was because in February of that year, the EU inspectors found that the expensive system of boluses inserted into the animals' second stomach, which the Department of Veterinary Services and BMC used to track cattle "from the farm to the dinner plate," was not up to standard. It would take eighteen months to unfreeze exports to Europe, costing Botswana's beef industry nearly half its revenue during that period.

The beef from the FMD-infected districts could not be sold to the EU. It could only go to places where the disease was already present. But it had to go somewhere. By the time of the 2011 outbreak, two decades after being exterminated entirely in the face of bovine pleuropneumonia, the cattle population in Ngamiland was an estimated 400,000 to 500,000—double the carrying capacity of the district. Amassing cattle at such a scale requires the regular slaughter of grown animals to make room for still-growing ones. In other words, this system to maximize growth is predicated on mass death—so Botswana had to find a home for this beef.

Botswana did what many developed countries do when they have excess commodities—especially those of poor quality or produced within state-subsidized industries. They sold them to their less fortunate "friends." In October 2011, Falepau announced he'd found a solution. The BMC had negotiated a plan to send sixty thousand live cattle from Ngamiland to Zimbabwe for slaughter in its abattoir at Bulawayo. Other cattle would be slaughtered in the Ngamiland abattoir at Maun for export to Angola, or transported live to Angola once storage facilities there were available.[31]

Eventually some twenty-six thousand animals were slaughtered at the government-owned cold-storage facility in Bulawayo. The beef was then marketed locally at subsidized prices by the Zimbabwean government, which was still trying to rebuild the economy and its food supply from its collapse a few years previously. According to the South African newspaper *The Citizen*, "The deal also included the supply, free of charge, of FMD vaccines by the Botswana Vaccines Institute (BVI) up to the end of 2015." Yet as of 2016 the Zimbabwean government had failed to pay its P1 million bill and the Botswana parliament was divided as to whether to cancel the debt altogether or continue to demand repayment. Meanwhile, the Zimbabwean government struggled to control yet another outbreak of FMD in the provinces that border Botswana.[32] The vaccine, the fence, the slaughterhouse, all worked in concert to support the conversion of cattle to beef, which is, in turn, its own technobiological input to human consumers.

The Taste of Growth

Throughout the colonial period, cattle were eaten only reluctantly beyond special, ritual occasions. In the early 1970s elderly men told Alverson they sold cattle to the abattoir "as a desperate measure dictated by 'need.' . . . They still consider the selling of a cow as a sign of 'failure.'"[33] Others sold occasionally to support school fees or other expenses, and some seniors saw the sale of an animal as part of helping that junior buyer to establish his own herd.[34] But soon the abattoir would become the purpose, the life destination for the bovine animal. For the slaughter-house to operate, and the beef industry to grow, the partible cow needs to be parceled to different markets. The contemporary bovine remains partible, but its flesh is now distributed far and wide, engendering a new, alienated bovine-human sociality. If the cow or the ox once contained a map of the family, now each animal maps a global economic landscape of trade and consumption. Desire has shifted from possession to ingestion, and the cow would now be scattered in pieces across the planet.

The EU market to which Botswana works so hard to retain access is not for the total animal. While local butcher shops in Botswana slaughter a cow or ox and sell all the cuts of meat for the same price per kilo, the global market imposes a value system on different parts of the animal and the EU grades beef to which prices are calibrated in relation to a set of criteria evaluating fat cover and carcass shape on the animal before slaughter. Botswana sends only boneless cuts of beef to Europe, both chilled and frozen. Removing bones and lymph nodes makes shipments lighter for transport but also reduces the risk of transmitting bovine spongiform encephalopathy (BSE, or mad cow disease). This disease has never appeared in Botswana. It was fostered in Britain through fattening practices in which herbivorous cattle were turned into carnivores, cannibalistic ones at that, through a diet supplemented with ruminant bone meal.

Within Europe, Botswana beef is then mainly sold to processors for conversion into institutional meals or mass-produced pub fare like steak and kidney pie. Boneless cuts, as well as bone-in and half carcasses, chilled or fresh, are also sold to South Africa and, to a lesser extent, Angola, Malawi, and other regional destinations. The hides of the cattle are tanned with chromium salts to the "wet-blue stage" and then sent to South Africa, Italy, Hong Kong, and China for further processing into leather goods. Bones and carcasses are processed by the BMC into blood meal, bone meal, and beef tallow, some of which is exported regionally. Offcuts are processed into canned corned beef, "polony" (the eerily bright pink cold cut sold in Botswana's supermarkets), and other processed meats by one of three local meat-processing companies.[35] Offal might be sold into the domestic supermarkets, or exported to South Africa. Beef by-products like lungs are processed into pet food and canned at a BMC subsidiary for export to South Africa. Horn is sold "to Japan and the UK, gall to France, hair to Germany, and gallstones to Hong Kong."[36]

The older mode of cattle keeping was organized around the rearing of oxen and dairy cows. One would be used for draught power, the other for milk and madila. Beef was the final stage of the bovine life course, but not its purpose. This occasional beef was cooked for many hours, stewed and pounded until soft, or perhaps sliced thin and cooked on a fire. Batswana, like other southern Africans, like their beef well cooked and expect it to be tough in texture. The new European market that has become the end goal of the BMC, by contrast, envisioned steak with a birth certificate and an accelerated life cycle designed to produce the tender beef that Europeans desire and might consume still bloody. Europeans and Americans like young animals, fattened on the feedlots, even as they wax nostalgic for the taste of "natural grass-fed" beef.

The push to sell and slaughter animals at much younger ages to serve European taste was only one element of the change from cattle to beef as a mode of interspeciation. The "sweet gravy" or "liquid food" enshrined in so much poetry was drying up. Madila—that staple of Setswana cuisine still ubiquitous in the 1970s—began disappearing, as did fresh milk. Calves grew faster if they fed on demand, and cows were called on to reproduce more rapidly, so milking was discouraged. As more children headed to schools, many families lacked the labor power necessary to organize milking. By the 1990s dairy had transformed from a staple food to a luxury item, with expensive powdered and boxed milk now sold in supermarkets and consumed in small quantities with tea. Holiday visits to the family cattle post, that repository of the moral imagination, were now punctuated with the nostalgic taste of fresh milk and madila. Though poorer households could not afford such things, beef would come to replace madila as a staple for Botswana's booming middle class.

In order for beef to continue its growth—in other words, in order for development to proceed—people have to eat the cow in parts. British pubgoers and Norwegian schoolchildren are not enough. Batswana too must eat beef. Consumption and growth are two sides of the same coin. In a report analyzing how to jumpstart beef industry growth after a period of stagnation, published jointly by the Botswana Ministry of Agriculture and the UN FAO in 2011, the authors project that Botswana's domestic beef market "will grow to over 40,000 tonnes of bone-in beef by 2022, i.e., it will absorb an additional 14,000 tonnes per year—roughly 70,000 head of cattle [over its current size]."[37] The domestic market has now surpassed the export market.

Public health nutritionist Lemogang Kwape describes a transformation of the diet under way in Botswana. A study of diet among elderly Batswana carried out in 1998 found that their diet centered on staple foods like sorghum and maize porridge. By contrast, Kwape's 2012 research found that the top five commonly consumed items among urban Batswana were tomatoes, sugar, beef, white bread, and brown bread. Sixty-three percent of his respondents ate beef at least twice a week.[38]

Globally the demand for beef continues to escalate at a dizzying rate of approximately 10 million tons per decade. Even as wealthier Europeans or North Americans fearing the risk of cardiovascular disease or colon cancer might begin to cut back on beef consumption, the global south middle classes and the urbanizing working classes will absorb the difference and then some. The taste of beef, in other words, is the taste of development.[39] Botswana is currently seeking access into the Chinese market for tripe and offal.[40] Consultants are also promoting Russian, North African, and Middle Eastern markets for Botswana beef.

The taste of beef is also the taste of a class-differentiated profit model. The bovine tissue used to make polony is from different grades and cuts of beef than the "ladies rump" sold at the Apache Steer Steakhouse in Gaborone's Riverwalk Mall and yet different from the "grass-fed organic hanger steak" sold in upscale British restaurants. And of course, the grass-fed organic hanger steak eaten in a European bistro tastes and chews quite differently from the older ox who, while never called "grass-fed" or certified as organic, roamed and grazed on Botswana's high-

Consume cattle to feed population

veld before being slaughtered and hung outside a local butchery. Each of these beef products is processed differently, from the "birth of the sirloin" through to its death, chemical enhancement, and seasoning. This technobiologically produced class-difference in taste underpins the paradoxes of the beef market such that even as the government parastatal BMC works to expand its market access, Botswana also spends ever more on imports of processed beef (importation of nonprocessed beef is still banned).[41] This is part of an economic vision promoted by consultants from the FAO and others. Because the imports are of processed beef, made from of a cheaper, lower grade than that exported, they argue that "importing cheap, lower-quality beef may free up more high-quality Botswana beef for sale to high-income consumers in the domestic, regional and global markets."[42]

Meanwhile, beef is being celebrated as a form of cross-generational leisure for the burgeoning middle class. Marshaling beef (notably—versus cattle) as a symbol of "traditional" Tswana culture, the past few years have seen the staging of "Beef Festivals" in Botswana as a cultural event for the middle class. For two hundred pula, those attending the Kgatleng Meat Festival in Morwa in April 2016 would be treated to an array of current music headliners like Charma Gal and Vee, a biltong (beef jerky) tasting, as well as plenty of meat cooked into a variety of dishes. With events throughout the day programmed for children and the elderly, attendees were advised to "bring their stomachs."[43]

Self-Devouring Growth

If cattle are interspeciated human familiars, as Batswana know them to be, perhaps it's not surprising that the growth of the cow has also seen the growth of the human. While approximately one in four households are still reported to be food insecure, obesity rates have risen precipitously in Botswana, particularly among women.[44] Cattle and humans are growing in tandem. But growth, it seems, is also about death. Cattle become beef only through slaughter. And then humans must consume more and more beef for growth to be realized. As the cycle of consumption escalates, new forms of death emerge.

The growth of beef is also part of the "slow death" of humans that Lauren Berlant describes.[45] Beef alone does not account for changes in human health. Contemporary diets include increased consumption of sugar, oil, and processed foods; there is a great deal of chicken alongside the beef. What I am suggesting here is not a simple causative relationship. Rather the hermeneutics of the cow was part of a certain kind of feeding/eating that underpinned the seasonal fluctuations of rural life, the hearth of extended families, and a calendar punctuated with ritual occasions. It was a world where people walked, sometimes great distances, sometimes with cattle. Beef, on the other hand, is part of the new landscape of restaurants, takeaways, and food vendors. It marks a shift to nuclear families provisioned at supermarkets to which people drive or ride, to children who eat off their own plates rather than out of a shared basin.

Batswana had long known that the well-being of cattle and that of humans were mirrored as interspeciated familiars. This is a brilliant insight. Perhaps it is not surprising then to note that elderly cattle are less valuable than they once were, just as elderly humans have lost some of their earlier prestige. The acceleration of the bovine life course is mirrored by the acceleration of the human life course.[46] Nor is it surprising to see the fattening of cattle and the fattening of humans occurring in tandem. In the past, during times of great hunger, cattle too lost their flesh. Mirroring the cow with its antibiotic-altered microbiome, carcass conformation, and fat cover, the human being also is shifting shape and composition. According to the WHO, obesity rates have risen precipitously, doubling globally in the period since 1980. By 2014 more than 1.9 billion adults and 41 million children were overweight or obese.[47] As the cow is immobilized, journeying by truck, so too are the people in their cars and minibus taxis.

Berlant calls slow death "the physical wearing out of a population and the deterioration of people in that population that is very nearly a defining condition of their experience and historical existence."[48] That process has been unfolding in Botswana under the sign of beef as the total social fact of development and

growth. In the late 1990s when I did research on debility in Botswana, I found many older people debilitated by hypertension,
diabetes, poststroke hemiplegia, and increasingly cancer. When
I returned in the mid-2000s to do new research, I found these
problems had only accelerated. Hospitals had set up weekly
hypertension clinics; a cancer ward had opened in the central
referral hospital, PMH. Private clinics and hospitals were offering dialysis, and eventually the Ministry of Health would open a
dialysis unit in PMH. By 2014 cardiovascular diseases accounted
for 18 percent of all deaths in Botswana, and diabetes a further
4 percent.[49]

Even as the taste of beef is cultivated and reshaped from
Germany to China to Botswana, with some 57 million tons consumed worldwide in 2016, the unfortunate fact is that too much
beef is deadly. Beef is only one element in a massive change in
consumption patterns across the globe over the past several decades, accompanying urbanization and new markets in food.
Food combines with changing patterns of physical activity,
chemical intake and exposure, and sleep to remake bodies. But
beef even as a single element in this shifting ecology is technobiological. Wherever parts of the globally dispersed cow land,
the clusters of obesity, diabetes, and cardiovascular disease seem
to grow.[50] Processed meats, of the type that Botswana beef often
becomes in Europe, and of the type that many poorer consumers
can afford, are particularly pathogenic.

In Botswana the effects of the shift from hunger to satiety,
from a desire to possess to a desire to consume the cow, means
that between 1980 and 1998 rates of hypertension increased five-
fold, and a 2009 study found that 67 percent of people over the
age of fifty had hypertension, while 12.3 percent had diabetes.[51]
New studies suggest that about 33.1 percent of Batswana have
both hypertension and diabetes, a co-morbid pattern that is particularly challenging.[52]

The cattle are drinking down the water table—a process with no end in sight. It turns out they are also evaporating the surface water.[53] Methane from belching, farting bovines, it seems, is a side effect of beef production. As anthropologist Radhika Govindrajan explains, "Methane emissions from livestock contribute about 80 percent of agricultural CH_4 and 35 percent of total anthropogenic methane emissions. . . . The explosive growth in the global population of cattle, driven by the seemingly insatiable craving for dairy and beef, is producing devastating effects on the planet. Human intervention and appetite has transformed flatulence from life into death, from a sign of the normal functioning of digestion to a sign of a planet in trouble."[54] Though since 2012 they are no longer used in Botswana's feedlots in keeping with EU regulations, the antibiotics used in many places, as part of the system of hygiene and growth used to convert cattle into global beef, have also been transforming the bovine microbiome into a more methane-rich environment. New research suggests that cattle who receive antibiotics produce more greenhouse gases.[55]

Of course, it is not only bovine flatulence that is contributing to the heating of the veld and the parching of Botswana. Turning cattle into beef for the global marketplace also means that those same cattle cannot travel "on the hoof." EU regulations require them to be shipped on trucks, even though this makes it more likely for an animal to fall and bruise or break a leg during the regular processes of loading and unloading that are required, and even though it is presumably quite stressful for the animals. Animals are immobilized, and yet their flesh, once cut, chilled or frozen, is sent great distances, even as other, lower grade beef from elsewhere cows is sent in the other direction, imported into Botswana. This paradox is not unique to Botswana. So too in Europe, and in the United States, Japan, and elsewhere, beef is exported even as it is imported. The entire process of distributing and redistributing the cow through the trade in flesh creates its own waste, the belching and farting of carbon dioxide and myriad toxins, warming the veld and dispersing and dirtying the rains.

Meanwhile, the growth of the national herd since the 1950s has meant an expansion of cattle into the Kalahari sandveld, a delicate ecosystem. As ranchers sank boreholes in the desert, more and more cattle were moved west, degrading the range in the process. As fences were erected to prevent the transmission of disease, wildlife was also prevented from migrating, and wildlife families have been separated, despite attempts by animals to reunite with their kin. This process has sometimes caused mass death from dehydration, particularly among fellow grazing herbivores like tsesebe, buffalo, zebra, and wildebeest.[56] The reduction in the population of these herbivores who browse (eating the woody stalks and stems of brush) more than cattle do combines with the increase in grazing cattle to change the biodiversity of the plant life in the sandveld, increasing desertification and eroding already delicate pasture.

From Hunger and Thirst and Back Again?

These health challenges are real, and yet an even deeper problem lies on the farther shore, after the carnivorous feast has ended. At one time every cow, bull, or ox had a kinship network, one that wove in and out of the kinship network of human familiars. Now every sirloin has a birthday, but not a name. What is the metaphysical status of cattle now? Who are they within this accelerated cycle of growth and death? What is it that humans are consuming when they eat Botswana beef? And what does it mean when humans kill cattle by the thousands or even the hundreds of thousands, dispersing their flesh to far-flung corners of the globe to be consumed by strangers, all in the interest of growth as a mode of wealth? This is not the sacrifice that was once made ritually, sparingly, in order to heal, to strengthen, to effect change in the material world. Nor is this the same as the historical mode of exchange that knit the world together through the movement of bovine familiars.

What kind of health is envisioned and created through the

industrialization of beef? As interspeciated familiars, the future of cattle is the future of people. Cattle, the ur-category of wealth and the basis of ritual, have always been central figures in Tswana political, social, and economic life. As modes of affiliation and patronage, technologies of metaphysical and material production, and aesthetic beings of tremendous regard, cattle have always been necessary to creating futures. But over time, they've been demystified, rationalized, rendered as beef. Through the rise of the beef industry within the developmental state, cattle have become figures of economic development, the subject of intense technoscientific management, and for many Europeans who consume Tswana beef, as well as their Batswana counterparts, a more regular part of the diet. The health effects of the transformation from cattle to beef—from the slow draining of the water table from cattle-watering boreholes, to the emission of methane and carbon, to the long-term effects of regular beef consumption—point toward a system of growth that is also a system of death. When the water and the pasture are gone and the cattle grow lean, when only those wealthy few command all the herds, the past hunger of the many may well return.

run its course

Cattle to Beef

A Photo Essay of Abstraction

The photographs collected here show the abstraction of cattle into beef. This is a process undertaken regularly in many places around the world, but these pictures are from Botswana. Most were taken by anthropologist Jacqueline Solway in 2007, inside the modern abattoir in Lobatse. The skilled workers maintain the high international standards of hygiene that are necessary to produce beef for the global market and domestic consumption.

Cattle crossing the road.
COURTESY OF GEORGE LAMSON.

Cattle in a lot.

(*opposite*) Cattle funneled into the vaccination line.
COURTESY OF INTERNATIONAL LIVESTOCK RESEARCH INSTITUTE.

(*above*) Vaccinating a cow.
COURTESY OF INTERNATIONAL LIVESTOCK RESEARCH INSTITUTE.

Killing floor at the abattoir.
COURTESY OF JACQUELINE SOLWAY.

Preparing to remove the hide.

Removing the hide.

The headless, skinless cattle are now beef ready for butchery.
COURTESY OF JACQUELINE SOLWAY.

Organ removal.

Offal on the conveyor belt.

Hanging sides of beef.

Racks of beef sides.

Removing cuts of beef from the sides.
COURTESY OF JACQUELINE SOLWAY.

Almost empty carcasses.

Vacuum-packaged beef on the conveyor belt.

COURTESY OF JACQUELINE SOLWAY.

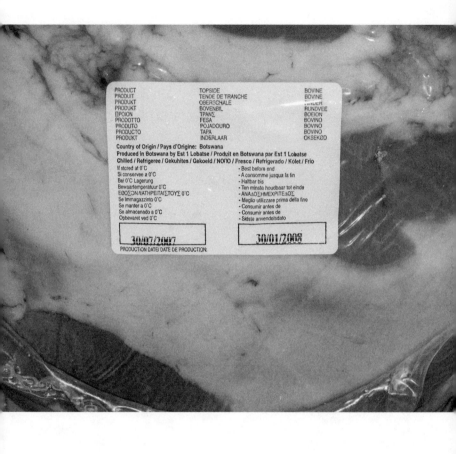

A single packaged topside of beef.

Boxing up the vacuum packages for shipping.
COURTESY OF JACQUELINE SOLWAY.

Boxes of chilled, packaged beef ready for export.
COURTESY OF JACQUELINE SOLWAY.

A worker in front of the EU cold storage.

Packaged meals of cooked, pounded beef for sale in a Gaborone supermarket.
COURTESY OF MICHAEL MAYER.

3

Roads, Sand,
and the Motorized Cow

They paved paradise and put up a parking lot.
—Joni Mitchell

THE FAIRY TALE OF BOTSWANA'S spectacular postindependence growth is often told as an unwitting haiku:

At independence
Botswana had only twelve
Km of tarred road

Now it has over seven thousand. This pithy little story appears in the preface to all manner of publications about Botswana: government websites, tourist guides, social science tomes, NGO reports, nostalgic memoirs. I myself have opened many a talk with this telling image. Sometimes it is said there were only six or seven kilometers of tarred road at independence; sometimes it is said there are eight thousand now. Such minor inconsistencies don't undermine the self-evident rags-to-riches character of the accomplishment. What better sign of economic growth than the steady proliferation of tarred roads crisscrossing the enormous expanse of desert and veld? From the Autobahn to the Los Angeles Freeway to the Trans-Kalahari Highway, roads are the sine qua non of development. These roads are necessary to transport the goods and labor required for consumption. Their pres-

roads = development

ence unleashes that central figure of self-devouring growth—the automobile.

Roads are fractal in nature, with branching constellations. So too is this parable, which contains parabolas within parabolas. Prepare yourself for a meandering journey. The lessons you will find along this journey are not simply antiroad. As though one could be! The road is a paradox. It can be a pathway to freedom or form the architecture of segregation.[1] Roads are vital and bring many good things—from ambulances, to visitors, to relief for those tasked with moving heavy loads. They are also modes of carnage.

Roads are part of the groundwork necessary for growth. But roads entail a reworking of landscape that is not immediately obvious, exceeding the goals of the engineers and planners who make them. Some of these side effects are self-devouring. Yet this modern mode of travel allows us to only barely notice the worlds we pass en route to our destinations. In this dreamy mode of barely noticing, devouring becomes easier.

Last spring, I attended a panel at Columbia University. The first speaker was the brilliant Michi Saagiig Nishnaabeg scholar and artist Leanne Betasamosake Simpson. She had arrived that afternoon in New York by plane from Toronto. She said she had spent the short flight imagining how her ancestors would have traveled the same journey from their territory on the north shore of Lake Ontario in spring by canoe. It would have taken many days. They would have visited the neighboring Haudenosaunee territory, where they would have renewed their social and political relationships through the sharing of food and ceremony. They would have provisioned themselves in part through the landscape they traversed with the permission of their neighbors. "We would have come out of the journey different than we went in," she observed. This transformative quality of the journey—its knowledge-making potential with its renewal of social and political life and its intimacy with the animated ecology—is effaced by the tarred road. Or think of the commuters crawling along the Cross-Bronx Expressway, the tarmac child of that great dam builder, Robert Moses. Such a road allows those in their cars to not know the people whose lives are lived outside the car window—the loss of neighborhoods, the asthma, the poverty the road begat.[2]

Perhaps it is not surprising that the first and biggest of Botswana's roads was brought by the growth of beef and converges at the town of Lobatse, where the slaughterhouse lies. Nowadays even more roads lead to Gaborone. The ever-growing capital city, built along with its dam at independence, eclipsed Lobatse in commercial importance some decades ago. Upon occasion when driving, there is the impressive and sudden appearance of the armored diamond-carrying vehicle with its security detail, plowing down the road toward the Debswana diamond sorting facility. More often there are buses and combis (minibus taxis operating set routes), private cars and pickup trucks, and lorries and government vehicles of all kinds. The roads link the major towns and villages of the country. They connect Botswana with its neighbors—and with distant ports on the Atlantic and Indian Oceans. They enable the referral hierarchy on which Botswana's health system is predicated, with ambulances and private vehicles transporting patients from small clinics to primary, district, and eventually tertiary hospitals.

Traversing the roads is an ever-expanding fleet of motorized vehicles. In 1966 there were 4,302 registered vehicles in a newly independent Botswana. By 2014 this number had risen exponentially to 435,750, and it shows no signs of slowing.[3] More cars means there is a need for more roads, in an ever-escalating cycle of transport-organized consumption. The roads themselves are central assets of the state. By 2011 Botswana's roads were valued at some 15 billion pula.[4]

This highway system is quite an accomplishment, as the many people who live in countries lacking such infrastructure can attest. But fairy tales inevitably have their dark sides. In Botswana, postindependence growth manifest in the tarred road is also regularly told as a lurid news story, complete with color photos. This is a spectacle in which the cow may make an appearance as in the story partially excerpted below, which appeared in one of Botswana's leading private daily newspapers in 2004.

HORROR CRASH IN SLEEPY VILLAGE

RADISELE: At least six passengers died on Tuesday evening when a northbound public service bus carrying 50 people collided with a truck near Radisele village. Residents of the relatively quiet and traditional village were shocked by wailings and flashes of red and blue lights from the police vehicles and ambulances at the scene of the accident about three kilometers outside the village.

"It was tense and scary as the police struggled with cutting torches to rescue the trapped body from what remained of a truck that was damaged beyond repair," said Tsietsi Solomon, who went to the scene of the accident just after it occurred. Solomon said there was an explosion that was followed by cries of human beings in desperation. "There was blood all over the scene, and we could see that the accident was very bad as the five-ton truck that collided with a bus was reduced to a scrap," he said.

He said what he saw at the scene suggested that one of the two vehicles must have been moving very fast. "Scrap metals from the truck were spread all over and actually nothing remained of the truck. At least, the bus was badly damaged on one side only." Solomon witnessed faces of pain and suffering. "They screamed, and shouted for help as the police worked hard to save lives."

Mahalapye police station commander, Superintendent Alakanani Makobo told Mmegi that six people died, and 16 passengers sustained serious injuries.

"Our initial investigations show that the bus hit a cow and apparently lost control before it collided with an oncoming truck which was going in the opposite direction," explained Makobo.

The stray cow, the bus with its sleepy passengers, the five-ton truck, the impatient drivers, and the screeching ambulance, like the flush toilet, the hair salon, and the polony sandwich, are all regular manifestations of growth that is premised on consumption. So too are the hours spent inhaling exhaust fumes while idling in thickets of gridlock during Gaborone's peak traffic hours. One July, in 2009 I think it was, I recall talk of a plague of carjacking in the city. Fearing for their safety and that of their vehicles, drivers were no longer stopping at the traffic lights after the sun went down, creating a free-for-all of sorts each evening.

Roads have always been a necessary element of long-distance trade and the regional economy of southern Africa. But roads have also become the thread that binds together the web of self-devouring growth. Roads orchestrate the total system of consumption. They set beef in motion as trucks haul immobilized cows toward the slaughterhouse. They spawn the planned communities complete with swimming pools and even golf courses that belie Gaborone's location on the desert's shore. They create an ever-expanding commuting class, bringing piped water into their peri-urban village homes, a class whose passion for the automobile would come to rival the cow, displacing it as the paradigmatic object of desire.

Mobility/Immobility

Most people in Botswana travel by road. As the road network grows, so does the volume of traffic, at the rate of 10 percent per year according to the Roads Department.[5] Tarred roads are meant to facilitate movement at speeds that greatly exceed that of pedestrians. Yet even from within the comfort of a private car, one cannot take speed for granted. With increasing traffic, the source of mobility also becomes a site of immobility. From 1981 to 2001 the traffic accident rate more than tripled, and it has remained high.[6] Between 2004 and 2011 there were nearly 150,000 car crashes, each one bringing a journey to a sudden halt. Accidents bring the road to a standstill. So do construction projects meant to expand it.

The road can hurt. Within the course of several hours on 9 and 10 September 2016 an elderly blind man, chief of a northern village, lost his wife, daughter, son, and grandson to a pair of collisions hundreds of kilometers apart. The first accident happened just after 2:00 p.m. on a Friday afternoon in the Bontleng neighborhood of Gaborone. A thirty-five-year-old man, son of the chief in question, lost his life while sitting in his VW

Golf GTI at a traffic light. A truck carrying a load of sand overturned after swerving to avoid a Mazda that had run a red light.
The VW and its driver were crushed and buried. Sand was everywhere. An ambulance arrived to take the driver of the Mazda to
the hospital. Traffic was snarled for hours as workers struggled to
clear the aftermath. Hours later, some five hundred kilometers
to the north, near the Zimbabwe border, his relatives were be-
side themselves to learn of the accident that had killed this
young man. The deceased's older sister, mother, and four-year-
old nephew, who had been visiting in a nearby village, began the
drive to their home, presumably to rejoin family and begin tending to the necessary mourning arrangements. The Toyota van
in which they were driving overturned. The mother and sister
were killed on the spot, while the small boy was transported to
the hospital in Francistown, where he later died.[7] Two accidents.
Three generations. Four deaths.

The loss here is unfathomable. Yet these kinds of unbear-
able tragedies are regular events in Botswana and beyond. In
November 2015, shortly after writing their national qualifying
exams, seven students died and over a hundred were injured
when the truck carrying them overturned after its tire burst on
the Molepolole-Kang road, just east of Dutlwe. As the nation
mourned, many angrily pointed to the political conditions that
left students transported in the backs of open trucks "like cattle"
while members of parliament rode in Mercedes cars.[8] A few
months later, in July 2016, five backup dancers for pop sensa-
tion Charma Gal returning from a performance died on the
same road, also following a burst tire. One could go on; the list
of high-profile accidents is seemingly endless. From politicians
and professional football players to nurses, teachers, construction workers, and church ladies, it seems everyone knows someone lost to the road. That the dead and injured are often young
compounds the stunning nature of the event.

By 2017 many thousands of people and an incalculable number of animals had died on Botswana's roads since the birth of the
modern road network. The road does help extend the mobility
of those debilitated persons who can access transportation. This
is an important contribution. But serious head or spinal injuries

incurred on the road had also left many people stuck in place. Botswana, like many countries, is a place where access to technical aids like wheelchairs and prosthetics is laborious and uncertain, while public transportation and public space, like buildings and sidewalks and paths, are often inaccessible by persons with disabilities. I recall accompanying a wheelchair user in the mid-1990s to the Motor Vehicle Accident Fund (MVA Fund) office in Gaborone, where she was pursuing a claim for support after the car accident that crushed her spine. The MVA is Botswana's national automobile insurance scheme, funded through a tax at the petrol pump (a clever idea!). Presumably this was an office where people with mobility impairments might be expected to visit regularly, given that road accidents are often debilitating. Yet we had to bring this woman to the city from a neighboring village in the back of my pickup truck and leave her seated there as we, carrying bits of paper necessary for processing her claim, ran up and down the stairs to the MVF office, which had been placed on the third floor of a building lacking a lift. That was two decades ago, but despite the construction boom, disability access remains a problem throughout Botswana. Meanwhile, like the funeral homes that blossomed during the height of the AIDS epidemic, and the security companies that have shadowed the expansion of conspicuous urban consumption, the panel beater (the body shop in American parlance) has become a booming business sector amid the ubiquitous spectacle of the road accident.

Excessive speed, intoxication, overloaded cars and pickups, poorly maintained vehicles including bald tires or poorly retreaded ones—both of which can blow on Botswana's scorching hot bitumen—as well as the tendency for cattle, goats, and wild animals to wander onto the tarmac without warning, all contribute to the dangers of the road. Over the years many studies have been done, and many public awareness campaigns and public safety programs launched.[9] The rate of accidents has risen and fallen by degrees. But in Botswana and throughout the world, the road remains a deadly place.

Even those on foot are vulnerable.[10] The road snatches children without warning. In 2014, 144 pedestrians were killed by automobiles on the streets (or sidewalks) of New York City, including several children. In 2016 the speeding convoy of Samantha Power, U.S. ambassador to the United Nations, struck and killed Birwe Toussem, a seven-year-old boy, in Cameroon. The convoy kept driving, as is their security protocol, but they dispatched one of the ambulances they travel with to tend to the corpse. No doubt the driver and everyone in the convoy and the village in which it occurred was devastated by this killing. Power insisted on returning days later to offer her condolences to the boy's family. Eventually the U.S. government gave this family 1 million Central African francs (approximately USD 1,700) as compensation for the loss of their child, as well as "two cows, hundreds of kilograms of flour, onions, rice, salt, sugar and cartons of soap and oil." In addition, the State Department planned to sink a well in the Toussems' village for drinking water.[11] These riches could come only through such a singular event—a moment when self-devouring growth revealed itself to powerful people. The reparations, of course, likely totaled far less than the sticker price of the air-conditioned vehicle that crushed Birwe's small body.

Around the world, the WHO estimates that some 1.25 million people die in crashes each year. Road accidents are the leading cause of death for people aged fifteen to twenty-nine.[12] Ninety-four percent of all accidents occur in low- or middle-income countries, though these places account for only half of the global stock of registered vehicles.[13] Africa has more than double the rate of traffic-related deaths in Europe, with Botswana in the lead.[14] Health economists anticipate crashes as the predictable outcome—the expected side effect—of economic growth. The rate eventually levels off and then declines after per capita income reaches a certain threshold.[15] China currently has three times the road fatality rate per 100,000 population than Italy; Vietnam, like Botswana, has four times more.[16] In East Germany, during the first two years of German reunification, the sudden expansion of the economy was accompanied by a quadrupling of the mortality rate from road accidents.[17]

It is ironic that Power was traveling with an ambulance. An

ambulance is a very good reason to have a road. But they are in short supply in Cameroon and across the global south, where the road can hurt but the hospital often fails to heal. In fact, people in lower- and middle-income countries are much less likely to survive traumatic injury than people in wealthier contexts. What good is a road if there is no ambulance, and what good is an ambulance when the hospital cannot keep people alive? Historically, public health attention focused on infectious disease and malnutrition. In recent years, road accidents and chronic illness have gained new attention. The United Nations has declared 2011–2020 as the Decade of Action for Road Safety, spawning a large WHO-led campaign. But this does not translate into trauma care, which is expensive, predicated on existing hospital and transportation infrastructure (roads! and ambulances), the presence of adequate hospital staff and material supplies, and the acquisition of technological capacity and training.

Take Botswana, for example. Botswana is typical of or perhaps even better off than many low- and middle-income countries in terms of trauma care capacity.[18] A decade ago, when I was an ethnographer in their central hospital, Botswana had ambulances in its national health service, and tarred roads for them to travel on. But these ambulances were designed and used to transport patients between levels in the referral system—that is, from village clinic to primary hospital to tertiary hospital. Their drivers were not trained in trauma care, nor were they equipped for or dispatched for that. And who would dispatch them? There was a small fleet of trauma-equipped ambulances that were owned and managed by a private emergency service for the small group of well-off urban or peri-urban people with private insurance or those who could pay out of pocket.

Trauma care requires a significant investment in high-tech equipment. Both Gaborone and Francistown have referral hospitals with accident and emergency departments that are equipped for trauma care, but staff often lack training, critical pieces of equipment may be missing or broken, and (at least a decade ago—this may have changed) they were not mainly run and envisioned as trauma centers so much as triaging sites. As for the rest of the health service—some sixteen primary and seven district hospitals—a study in 2007 described trauma capacity as follows:

> Generally, primary hospitals are basic facilities with a limited capacity for severe trauma care. Except for administration of oxygen, the skills for basic and advanced airway management and spine immobilization were limited, especially at the primary hospital level but also at the district hospital level. A total of 3 hospitals were not able to provide endotracheal intubation at all, and this service could be provided on a "sometimes" basis in 18. Recovery position was an unknown procedure in 11 hospitals. Chest tube insertion was a procedure that could be provided by all doctors caring for injuries in only 11 locations. . . . Control of external hemorrhage by deep packing was available on a 24-h basis in one hospital and "sometimes" in seven; wrapping potential pelvic fractures was available on a 24-h basis in one facility and "sometimes" in six.[19]

Before the tarred road, people walked many kilometers a day; now they drive or ride. These roads can be a terrific thing. In her fascinating social history of Nairobi's taxi business, Kenda Mutongi talked to women who remember how *matatus* (combis) relieved them of carrying crushing burdens. Over time, women's necks and backs had curved and bulged in stiffness and pain from years of carrying heavy loads.[20] For some elderly or otherwise debilitated people, riding opens new possibilities, and roads are built to mitigate some problems of porterage and mobility. And the ambulance must travel on the road if it is to help anyone.

But the road giveth and the road taketh away. The accident is not the only way that road travel can hurt. Roads are part of the public health vision enabling the ambulance, the medications, and the patients to travel. But in a world structured by the road, public health attention turns to the importance of walking. In clinics across Botswana middle-aged and elderly patients are being encouraged to walk. The sedentary rider, no less than the consumption of immobilized beef, helps account for the escalating rates of hypertension, heart disease, diabetes, and other chronic ailments in Botswana. As S. Lochlann Jain has argued, the self-devouring aspect of automobility is accepted as a necessary element of growth.[21]

Spaghetti junctions and bypass roads now under construction are a response to the immobility wrought by vehicular consumption. By 2012 the Botswana government was contemplating a staggered work schedule for the civil service and staggered school opening times in an effort to modulate the rush-hour traffic clogging greater Gaborone. From Cairo to Nairobi to Delhi to Los Angeles, car-owning commuters set out before dawn to beat the morning traffic, as perpetual road-construction perpetually fails to keep up with escalating road use. Together the car and the road offer a seesaw of stasis and speed, freedom and confinement.

Botswana built these roads as a public good. But roads are not the same thing as public transportation. Buses and minibus taxis that ply the roads are privately owned, and private companies control the routes. Botswana Airways is a parastatal, but it is currently for sale and air travel is necessarily priced well beyond the reach of most Batswana. The railway was owned and operated by Rhodesian Railways (later National Railways of Zimbabwe) from independence to 1986, when the government, with assistance from the Swedes, the Chinese, and others, founded Botswana Railways. But in 2009 they discontinued passenger service, only to reintroduce it in 2016, and as with the airlines, the route is limited and the cost of travel high.

Gaborone, whose sprawl has been vast, has no municipal buses or light rail or subways. The city had begun as a small administrative town in 1966, its dam dug and its road untarred. As the web of tarred roads leading to the city expanded, Gaborone consumed nearby villages, turning them into bedroom communities for the working poor and the aspirant. The tarred road also opened new land for upscale, gated communities like Phakalane, some fifteen kilometers north of the city center, with its water-hungry golf course, swimming pools, man-made reservoir, and air-conditioned hotel and clubhouse. While the working poor walk in the dusty heat or winter chill to their local combi stop, where they queue to pile into minibus taxis to ride to their low-wage service jobs, the aspirant, the middle class, and the wealthy eschew the crowded combis, preferring to sit in traffic in their own cars. The accident thus threatens not only the human body but also one of its prized possessions, the automobile.

The Road to Wealth

The road commands a certain amount of death and damage as a necessary price for its freedoms and opportunities.[22] But this is only the most immediately visible element of an extensive system of self-devouring growth that the tarred road portends. The very construction and presence of the tarred road quite literally reconstitutes the world.[23]

Roads are not new in southern Africa—this part of the world has long been mobile, with regional trade beginning millennia ago, and these movements were not chaotic, they followed established roads and paths. Much as politics has long revolved around water, wealth and sovereignty have also manifest as attempts to control the road. Chinese and Persian pottery found by archaeologists at the Great Zimbabwe site to the east of Botswana demonstrates that trade routes connected southern Africa to Asia as early as the fourteenth century, long before the arrival of Europeans. The Save River, which we will meet again, was such a road, flowing from Zimbabwe through Mozambique and emptying into the Indian Ocean. Gold and later copper were traded and within a few centuries, led by the Portuguese, the European consumption of Africans was under way, drawing captive people and trade goods on overland and seafaring routes to slave ports in Angola, South Africa, and Mozambique.

By the nineteenth century the Europeans had introduced the oxcart or wagon, which would become an iconic element of the Afrikaner mythos. Missionaries and other Europeans traversed Botswana in their wagons. Batswana too began carrying loads for exchange between villages and to the emerging European trading posts and cities in what would become South Africa. By the twentieth century Batswana, who also rode their oxen, were using wagons for carrying building materials and grain between their farms and village homes, and for attending weddings, funerals, and other social events.

With the onset of colonialism in 1885 the British channeled this movement for their own economic and political ends. They built a (privately owned) railway in 1897 connecting Southern Rhodesia to South Africa. The railway became a vacuum of sorts, sucking African men into the mines of the Witwatersrand. The mines were places that devoured many, eating through their breath, dwindling their bodies. They were also places that facilitated new kinds of consumption—from white sugar to wingtips. Feeder roads in turn led to the railway, which passed through the eastern corridor of Bechuanaland as the main carrier of goods and people between Southern Rhodesia and South Africa.

But though the Europeans introduced the wagons and eventually the railroad, Batswana sought to control the power and the danger of the road on their own terms.[24] Each year the roads leading into the capital villages were doctored and purified in a set of rituals meant to strengthen the polity and protect it from harm. Public wagon roads developed through repeated usage, as wheels wore tracks into the veld. The chiefs commanded labor regiments of men, organized by age grades, to maintain them, just as they sent regiments of women to maintain dams.[25] They forbade their people from plowing over these roads.[26] They regulated use with an eye for safety and traffic concerns, banning wagons on motor roads, or requiring proper brakes on wagons, for example.[27]

By the 1930s motorcars and lorries had begun to take over the work of wagons. Some were owned by the European trading posts, which grew in number as demand for consumer goods rose, while colonial policy barred Africans from acquiring their own trading licenses. The mine labor recruitment agency began a bus service carrying recruits and private passengers to the railhead. Chief Bathoen II of the Ngwaketse started his own private bus company. He recognized the power of the road and sought to monopolize it personally, a reflection of the increasing autocratic authority that accrued to Tswana paramount chiefs under British indirect rule. Anthropologist Ornulf Gulbrandsen offers the following story he was told in the 1970s:

> Radiputi was a senior member of [Bathoen's] *kgotla*, a person who people recalled as extraordinarily hard working, good with cattle and open minded: "He always wanted to try new things." In the 1950s he bought a bus and wanted to start a bus service between Kanye and the railway township of Lobatse. What then followed was told to me by many different people, and I relate it in the words of one of his friends: "Then Kgosi Bathoen became angry—he became in fact very jealous towards Radiputi. *He wanted to have the road for himself.* Radiputi had to retreat and start a far less attractive service between Kanye and Mafeking. Bathoen said that '*this is my road*, so just get away.' You know it was not really right of him to say that, because although in a certain sense we say that everything in the morafe [chiefdom] belongs to the kgosi [chief], this does not mean in such a personal sense—in the sense that he could take the advantage of it and run his own business. That was not right!"[28] (emphasis mine)

By 1944 there were 347 private and 308 commercial motor vehicles in the protectorate.[29] These prized possessions got stuck in the sand, in ditches, or in mud in the rainy season, just as wagons had. To read the correspondence and diaries of a mid-century missionary doctor is to bear witness to the pleasures, frustrations, and pains of the motorcar. Yet it quickly became untenable for European officials to arrive by any other means. Such was the status of the automobile.[30] Roads were tracks with wheel ruts made through repeated use. Grading and engineered road construction began in the late 1930s but was quickly halted by the onset of World War II, only to resume again in the 1950s.

As consumption of cars and trucks began to climb, the grading and paving of the roads became necessary. Vehicles cost money. They were significant investments that the ill-maintained road could destroy. At independence, road making became part of the developmental impetus, an infrastructural expectation of the modern nation-state. Just as chiefs had once attempted to control commerce and territorial sovereignty via the road, now the nation, which did not yet even own the railway that passed through its land, would seek the same.

Eventually, a highway system was built, the centerpieces of which were three highways that formed first a gravel and eventually a tarred ring around the perimeter of the country. The ring is joined to connector roads that lead to the border posts and beyond. This network would later be expanded with ancillary highways added and extra lanes in key sections of the main highways, and bypasses ringing major villages and the capital to ease congestion.

These roads, seen on any official map of the country, came under the oversight of the Ministry of Works and Communication (later Ministry of Transport and Communication). But by the late 1970s over 80 percent of Batswana still lived in rural villages, which were served by some thirteen thousand kilometers of ungazetted roads that fell under the decentralized control of the district councils.[31] These were tracks that wound through villages, connecting agricultural lands and cattle posts, and rural roads that linked smaller satellite villages. These were the sorts of roads that may not appear on a paper map but which a local could sketch into the sand with a stick when directing a visitor.

At one time the chain gangs infamously compelled to build the roads of Australia and Alabama were also to be found in southern Africa.[32] In the mid-nineteenth century, Sechele I, paramount chief of the Bakwena, wrote to the missionary David Livingstone that he had "adopted a mode of punishment he had seen [on a recent visit to the Cape Colony], namely making criminals work on the public roads."[33] But most roads were built and maintained through the use of regimental labor. At independence, the chiefs lost control over such labor, and in the 1970s rural (or ungazetted) road construction was reimagined under a new model of development. In development discourse the world over, roads have long been fetishized as the magic amulet that will end poverty, Botswana was no different. It was decided that the national hunger for roads would solve the national hunger for employment, sheltering and even lifting the poor, while growing the economy.

At the time, most roads in the country were still made of earth. While long-term plans envisioned the gazetted roads graded and eventually paved using heavy machinery, the rural roads would be hand-built by villagers. With technical and financial assistance from the International Labor Organization, Norway, and other partners, labor-intensive road building became a poverty alleviation program. This was in the 1980s, when over half of Botswana's population still lived below the poverty line. The South African mines had retrenched Batswana in the 1970s, and unemployment remained a perennial concern. Road building was poorly remunerated, but it meant tackling two development challenges—employment and infrastructure—at once.[34] The mines had only employed men, but women too, already the builders of homes and courtyards, would now work at road building in the new nation.

Gangs of villagers would be hired to work in teams under a trained leader, clearing stumps and brush, building drainage, and so forth. They would learn skills in road building and road maintenance, and receive a small income to supplement their farming. Public sector work has long been a critical source of employment in Botswana, accounting for some 30–40 percent of all formal jobs.[35] By 1990 over ten thousand people had been so employed, in increasingly mechanized methods. In that same year nearly nine hundred people had achieved long-term employment in the program, accounting for some 10 percent of the total civil service.[36]

In the 1980s road building also became part of a scheme most people call "drought relief," which politicians hoped might stem the tide of rapid urbanization to a city that could neither employ nor house newcomers nearly as fast as they arrived.[37] By the 1990s this was a permanent program that increased its enrollments during drought years. Drought relief included direct food transfers to approximately 60 percent of the population.[38] Even as boreholes and dams and piped water shifted the emphasis of water politics away from rainmaking and toward hydro engineering, so too road building and other public works projects, like the construction of rural schools, provided a limited livelihood and safety net when the rains failed. In 1992, at the height of another five-year drought, the Labour Based Drought Relief Programme employed some 189,000 people in temporary jobs.[39] Meanwhile, road building itself required vast quantities of water. _A_

The architects and analysts of drought relief understood consumption as its overarching rationale. Here is how one development consultant, based at the International Food Policy Research Institute in Washington, described it: "The relief program is an integral component of Botswana's development strategy. . . . The program aims to reduce inter-temporal fluctuations in consumption through the provision of income support, as well as to preserve assets and means of production to protect future consumption."[40]

A study published in 2004 showed that households in which someone participated in drought relief had more cattle (certainly not beef) than those that didn't. Building roads for cars helped some poor people hang on to their cattle.[41] Yet other benefits under the 1980s Drought Relief Programme included subsidies for borehole sinking and livestock feed that were regressive, benefitting the wealthy disproportionately. It brought subsidized tractors, those motorized oxen, for plowing, which required farmers to remove stumps and other vegetation that had anchored the topsoil. The tractor dribbled oil and shat carbon monoxide, unlike the cow whose dung had fertilized the field. Within Botswana, as within other regions afflicted by the severe droughts of the 1980s—California, Eastern Australia, and the African Sahel—the failure of the rains further consolidated the wealth of some even as many more lost their livelihoods. Even as drought relief brought new forms of infrastructure and development, "the percentage of farmers without cattle rose from 28 percent in 1980 to 39 percent in 1987."[42]

Development scholar Onalenna Selolwane explains that the end of the labor-intensive road-building program in the 1990s marked a shift in the technological maturity of infrastructure as well as a turn in the theory of development toward privatization. Dirt roads were no longer the goal. The Ministry of Works and Transport now sought to "bitumize" the gravel and earthen roads, grading them by machine and coating them in a petroleum by-product between layers of sand.[43]

moved away from dirt roads

Privatization brought international contractors into Botswana's road building in greater numbers, beginning in the 1990s. Up until then, European and South African firms had mainly been the ones to bring the necessary capacity for constructing a major roadway. But in the 1990s developing Botswana would become a significant source of profit for an expanding range of companies, from Kuwait to South Africa to China. The number and size of the roads has continued to grow, as has the sophistication of design. At present a "spaghetti junction" with looping on-ramps is nearing completion in Francistown (built by China Railways Group), highway segments are being widened with new lanes added, and in partnership with Zambia, Botswana has nearly completed a bridge at Kazangulu (built by Korean firm Daewoo) to connect the two countries by road, replacing the ferryboat that has long been the only way to cross the Zambezi River.

Botswana has long been known for keeping corruption to a minimum. Yet scandals have followed the Roads Department since privatization and the move to more complex and expensive projects. In 1998 the director of the Roads Department was convicted of corruption for accepting a 100,000 pula bribe from ZAC Construction when it was competing for the tender of the Rasesa–Monametsana road rehabilitation project in 1994. The owner of ZAC is Nicholas Zakhem, at the time a Lebanese businessman—he has since become a Motswana citizen—who also owns the Gaborone football team and is a major contributor to the ruling political party. The construction scandal resulted in the resignation of a cabinet minister, who has since resurrected his political career.[44] In 2012 new scandals had emerged that resulted in corruption charges against both the director and the deputy director of the Roads Department, after investigations revealed millions of pula spent in false claims that defrauded the government.[45] Soon it emerged that irregularities in the awarding of drivers' licenses and roadworthiness permits for vehicles were also a major source of corruption.[46]

Road construction contracts now run in the hundreds of millions of pula each. And as with construction everywhere—from Boston's Big Dig to the second bathroom I put in my apartment so that I could consume water in private without anyone pounding on the door to hurry up — costs often mushroom far beyond original estimates. From 2006 to 2016 the government spent over 5 billion pula in road construction, including nearly a billion in cost overruns.[47] Take, for example, the 108-kilometer road connecting the village of Kang in the Kalahari with the western village of Hukuntsi, complete with the 4.2-kilometer tarred loop within Kang, finished in 2012. This road was built by Chinese firm Sinohydro Botswana, who billed the Roads Department for 536 million pula (USD 82 million). Sinohydro eventually received some 75 million pula less than this amount after a series of high-profile scandals and struggles over delays and cost overruns.[48] This included accusations that the construction giant had bribed someone on the local land board for allocation of a quarry site, and conflict of interest between the consulting engineering company overseeing the project and the construction company.[49] The project engineer, meanwhile, blamed the lack of water and skilled labor in the region for the delays and ballooning costs.[50] Sinohydro was already under pressure for massive delays, cost overruns, and quality concerns on several other high-profile construction projects, including the expansion of Gaborone's Sir Seretse Khama International Airport, and the road between Francistown and the Zimbabwe border town of Ramokgwebana. The company has since folded and left Botswana.

Sand and Water

Building the road requires huge quantities of — you guessed it — water. It also needs aggregate and bitumen — a petroleum by-product. One could be forgiven for focusing on petroleum and water as the two finite resources at stake here in the politics of self-devouring growth.[51] But that would be a false move. It turns out that sand and gravel, or aggregate, as they are called in construction, are also finite resources; humans are using them faster than they can replenish. We are all living in sand castles now. Aggregate, the principal element in concrete, is the material substance from which urban development grows. Shopping malls in Gaborone, hospitals in Singapore, office buildings in Los Angeles, airports in Chengdu, apartment blocks in Manila, sports stadiums in New Jersey, and matchbox houses in Soweto are all made from concrete, and thereby from aggregate. Aggregate is used in the graded sub-base on which roads are laid, and it is then mixed into layers of bitumen or asphalt. And aggregate mining, like the cattle drinking from the borehole, is crucial to understanding how growth begets thirst. The fortunes of sand and water are conjoined.

As cities across the world "grow like a baby," as Batswana described Gaborone to anthropologist Mieka Ritsema, they consume aggregate voraciously.[52] In 2009 the concrete industry was the largest consumer of natural resources globally, consuming 1.6 billion tons of cement, 10 billion tons of aggregate, and 1 billion tons of water.[53] And of course, building projects use sand and gravel beyond the making of concrete. By 2017 more than 48 billion tons of aggregate were being used annually for construction.[54]

Botswana's escalating spiral of roads and cars is but one minor site in a global explosion of road building. Journalist David Owen puts this road-based relationship of self-devouring growth in perspective: "A mile-long section of a single lane of an American interstate highway requires thirty-eight thousand tons. The most dramatic global increase in aggregate consumption is occurring in parts of the world where people who build roads are trying to keep pace with people who buy cars. Chinese officials have said that by 2030 they hope to have completed a hundred and sixty-five thousand miles of roads — a national network nearly three and a half times as long as the American interstate system."[55]

The largest continual expanse of sand in the world stretches from South Africa to Congo-Brazzaville, traversing Botswana and covering two-thirds of the country.[56] But this kind of sand is not typically used for modern construction. Desert sand, formed by wind, is more uniform and round in shape than river or coastal sand or gravel. This prevents it from binding as well in concrete, threatening its long-term structural integrity. It is used as a graded sub-base in road construction but not mixed within the pavement layers. This is why the United Arab Emirates and Saudi Arabia, who would seem to have an overabundance of sand, have both imported sand from Australia to support ongoing development.

Marine sand, by contrast, formed by water, possesses the necessary irregular shapes but must be washed thoroughly to remove salinity that can corrode and weaken metal structures used to support concrete. River sand and gravel, from beds or quarries, has long been the preference for construction. But as construction rates escalate, this aggregate is in short supply. The depletion of aggregate from riverbeds and quarries has led to increased mining of coastal and marine sand, with perilous consequences for coastal erosion and ocean biodiversity.[57] Government regulations to protect dwindling sand reserves have been met with the rise of criminal gangs, fueling illicit sand mining and a thriving black market in, of all things, sand.[58]

In the late 1990s experts were promoting aggregate mining as having a "bright future" in Botswana. By 2013 an official from the Botswana Department of Geological Survey reported that demand for river sand had "increased dramatically over the past decade; generated by the high rate of development within the greater Gaborone area.... These developments need high tonnages of river sand mined illegally from the river beds all over Botswana to meet the demand.... The river eco-systems are deteriorating due to the prolonged extraction."[59] Sand miners, many of them working illegally, had dug so far into riverbeds that they had created new channels for runoff during the brief season when suddenly water flows through the otherwise dry rivers in Botswana's southeast.[60] As a result the riverbeds don't hold water as they used to, further depriving the dams downstream and contributing to water shortages.[61]

This problem is not unique to Botswana. Rivers are living systems, and aggregate mining can badly injure them, permanently altering the riverbed and the swath of land through which they are fed, altering pH levels, and increasing pollution. Potential effects of excess sand and gravel extraction can include "[an] increase in flood frequency and intensity by reducing flood regulation capacity" and an increase in drought, by precipitating a sinking of the water table and the drying up of tributaries.[62]

sand extraction →

Engineers in Botswana, in partnership with Norwegian engineers and others, have pioneered new techniques for using Kalahari sand in road making, and recently the Department of Roads has begun promoting this technology for use in low-volume roads.[63] And the government is also now looking into making aggregate by machine from a mix of rock mined at quarries in the country. But river-quarry sand and gravel were also once considered abundant. Perhaps if rock and desert sand are drawn into the heart of self-devouring growth, and construction companies begin molding shopping malls and roads out of them, they too will someday become scarce; they too will prove crucial to the uncertain flow of water.

Detour

I want to get to the car, that shiny object of desire hurtling down the road or parked on the bitumen outside the mall. But first let me take you on a little detour down the unseemly side of the road. I've decided against leading you through the petroleum chain, perhaps into Angola or Nigeria where oil flows thick and deadly long before it finds its way into bitumen or filling stations or the plastic wrapped around the packets of beef in the supermarket. The militarized, toxic, and predatory reaches of the carbon economy are well documented.[64] This detour will take us down less-frequented roadways, including some within the "green" economy.

Botswana is mainly a place where cars are consumed, not created, though there have been several attempts at vehicle assembly or parts, bringing badly needed jobs to a country whose unemployment rate hovers around 20 percent. Hyundai and Volvo operated assembly plants in Botswana for some years in the late 1990s. My part-time research assistant in 1999 was lucky enough to get work assembling wiring harnesses for them, and she promptly left my employ for this greener pasture only to be laid off a few months later. When I began to look at why both plants closed, I discovered a mini road empire.

Both of Botswana's vehicle assembly plants were part of the business holdings of white Zimbabwean entrepreneur Billy

Rautenbach, under the conglomerate of car dealerships, service stations, and assembly plants then called Wheels of Africa. By 2000 they were collateral damage in a tax fraud and embezzlement scandal in South Africa, which resulted in the seizure and liquidation of assets by creditors, including some USD 23 million of debt owed to the Botswana Development Corporation and a further USD 9 million to the First National Bank of Botswana.[65] Only a fraction of this and other monies owed was recovered by the piecemeal sale of Botswana's Hyundai plant.[66]

Rautenbach, a former racecar driver, is a "colorful figure" — which is a euphemism for the sort of white mercenary-entrepreneur who is the toxic afterbirth of southern African colonialism. At various moments, Rautenbach has found himself ejected from Congo, a fugitive from South Africa, blacklisted by the EU, a target of U.S. sanctions against Zimbabwe, and named in the Panama Papers for money laundering and tax evasion. Dubbed "the Napoleon of Africa," Rautenbach commands a vast and opaque empire predicated on the road. It began when he inherited a Southern Rhodesia–based transport company built by his father, who would later die in an accident on Zimbabwe's Harare–Chirundu road.[67] Under the son's control it grew into the biggest trucking company on the continent. This began with Rautenbach's acquisition and refurbishment of a phalanx of busted Volvo trucks, abandoned detritus after the war in Mozambique. Soon he had the Volvo distribution franchise for the region. After the collapse of Hyundai Botswana, Rautenbach, who had admitted to paying bribes in the past, was facing over three hundred counts of fraud and tax evasion in South Africa and was forced to flee the country. Nearly a decade later, he struck a deal with South African prosecutors and testified in the corruption trial of former South African national police commissioner and Interpol director Jackie Selebi.[68] After paying a substantial fine, Rautenbach, no longer a fugitive, was back in business in South Africa.

Meanwhile, the liquidation of many of Wheels of Africa's holdings during his period of exile did not seem to slow Rautenbach down. His business interests are continually in flux and hidden behind shell companies.[69] But at various times, in addition to trucking, he has imported and distributed construction equipment, and owned and operated farms and safari concessions in Zimbabwe, Kenya, Mozambique, and Congo.[70] A close associate of the Zimbabwean president, Emmerson Mnangagwa, Rautenbach has parlayed his influence with Zimbabwe's ruling ZANU-PF party into multiple endeavors.

According to exposés in the southern African press, in the mid-1990s Rautenbach began selling arms to the government of the Democratic Republic of Congo (and eventually the rebels fighting against them as well), in violation of an arms embargo. It is rumored that the arms were purchased from the weapons manufacture division of Daewoo, the South Korean conglomerate, a story that emerged when South African prosecutors implicated Rautenbach in the assassination of Daewoo South Africa CEO Young Koo-Kwon.[71] In 1998, despite his lack of experience, Rautenbach was named CEO of the Congolese state mining company GECAMINES (La Generale des Carriers et des Mines), as compensation to Robert Mugabe for Zimbabwean military support in Laurent Kabila's fight against Ugandan and Rwandan forces. Eventually, huge cobalt mining concessions were transferred to one of Rautenbach's holding companies, Ridgepointe International. This was a self-financing war economy, where huge amounts of mineral wealth were expropriated amid a thriving arms trade and substantial loss of life. Cobalt mining conditions in Congo were notoriously dangerous and brutal, consuming bodies both wholesale and piecemeal. But the substance itself was quite valuable as a component in the lithium-ion batteries of both cellular phones and that green promise of the future road—electric cars.

Daewoo was the second largest company in South Korea after Hyundai, a poster child of the explosive growth of the "Asian Tigers" until, in the wake of the Asian financial crisis, the Korean government disaggregated it, selling the car division off to General Motors in 2001. Given how deadly cars can be, perhaps it's not surprising that many car companies would also be manufacturing assault rifles and grenade launchers. The automobile industry and the "defense" industry, as it is called, are quite intertwined. Hyundai manufactures Elantra sedans and also heavy artillery. Subaru makes station wagons and also military aircraft for the Japanese defense agency. Jeeps and Humvees are military vehicles Americans drive to the mall. And Daewoo's shipbuilding division, which manufactures the enormous cargo ships that carry the substance of self-devouring growth around the globe, has recently partnered with Lockheed Martin to make combat ships.

In the early 2000s Rautenbach entered into a joint venture with the Mugabe government to develop an ethanol business back home in Zimbabwe. He was the recipient of ZANU-PF largesse in the form of control over a huge tract of land in Chisumbanje, in eastern Zimbabwe, on the shores of the Save River. He used this land to build a biofuels business called Green Fuel — growing sugarcane on a swath of land the size of Manhattan and building the largest biofuel processing plant on the continent, which began producing ethanol in 2011. Biofuels were of great interest to the Zimbabwe government. At the time it allocated the land to Rautenbach, Zimbabwe faced petrol shortages amid hyperinflation, a scarcity of foreign exchange, and a collapsing economy.[72] By 2013 Rautenbach had succeeded in pressuring the Zimbabwe government into mandating a biofuel-petrol blend at the nation's pumps and Green Fuel was attempting to make deals with Zambia, South Africa, Mozambique, Malawi, and Botswana for ethanol sales.[73]

Though the ethanol plant and associated cane plantations claimed to create 4,500 jobs, its establishment displaced many thousands of Zimbabweans who lost their farms or saw them drastically reduced in size. In Chisumbanje, women farmers who had long worked this land, in a place where women bore responsibility for feeding their households, were particularly hard hit. Unable to gain wage-paying jobs at the plant, some found new opportunities in petty trade or other businesses that sprang up around the facility. But many went hungry, as did their children. Meals were skipped; tummies felt hollow inside — in that aching, burning sort of way. Perhaps there were dreams of beef and great plates of porridge with sauce; perhaps tempers flared. Rates of kwashiorkor rose as fuel and food were pitted against one another in a zero-sum game in a country with ongoing food shortages.[74] In 2014, after appealing to Parliament, angry residents burned huge swaths of the cane fields in protest. Green Fuel began impounding their cattle in retribution after laying claim to what had long been communal grazing land. By 2015 some 500 plant workers had gone on strike, protesting that they hadn't been paid in seven months, along with 116 cane growers who complained they were owed three years of back pay.[75] Many others were bitterly aware that their promised jobs amounted to subcontracted piecework for extremely low pay.[76]

Ethanol is aggressively marketed as a clean fuel. But this plant and the irrigation channels for the cane drank vast quantities of water. In 2014, at the height of the drought that saw the evaporation of Gaborone's dam to the east, ZINWA (Zimbabwe's national water authority) cut the ethanol plant's water supply for two months over a USD 7 million unpaid water bill. Back online, it leaked toxic effluent into the water supply, which meandered down the Save and its tributaries, those ancient trade routes, headed toward Mozambique. Along the way it leached into fields and gardens. Animals, including cattle, died from drinking polluted irrigation water, and people complained of open sores on their feet and skin rashes. Some went partially blind.[77]

Meanwhile, the trucks hauling the cane destroyed the road, reducing it to potholes while also making it considerably more dangerous. Villagers protested that within a few years of the plant opening, fifteen children had been killed by company trucks laden with cane. The ethanol tankers were equally perilous, as was witnessed in 2013 when a Green Fuel tanker collided with a Mazda truck carrying a family of mourners, and twenty-two people in Chisumbanje died in a fireball fed by the explosion of ethanol.[78]

Zimbabwe's mandate was not unique. Energy independence and "renewable" energy have obvious appeal. By 2016 some sixty-four countries globally had mandated, or set targets for mandating, biofuel blending.[79] The land needed for biofuels either comes from virgin ecosystems (as in the clear-cutting of Amazon forest and its replacement with cane fields in Brazil, or the similar trend happening with oil palm in West Africa's Mano River Region), which can undermine benefits to result in a net carbon gain, or it needs to happen on existing agricultural land, which puts ethanol in competition with food supply, as happened in Zimbabwe, pushing food prices up.[80] And as in Zimbabwe, farmers then are pushed to clear new and often marginal lands to put into cultivation. Fertilizers, pesticides, and huge amounts of water are all needed to produce this "cleaner" fuel.[81] And as Patience Mutopo and Manase Chiweshe astutely note, land grabs are also water grabs.[82]

American readers familiar with the history of ethanol in our own country will recognize that Rautenbach is far from alone in his attempt to parlay political access into biofuel profits. And with land in short supply in high-consumption countries, across Africa there is a new land grab under way that threatens domestic food supplies and undermines local ecologies in a fit of self-devouring growth. In one of the most high-profile of such cases, the Korean firm Daewoo (just when you forgot about them — I know, it is almost like a Thomas Hardy novel) almost succeeded in renting out half the arable land in Madagascar to put into cultivation for biofuels and food for export. They were to acquire a ninety-nine-year lease, rent free, under the dubious justification that Malagasy would benefit from employment opportunities. When the public learned of this deal, they were furious, and staged mass protests that drove the government from power.[83]

Having detoured through this regional road empire following a smiling little Napoleon in his safari hat, we've seen that biofuels and lithium-ion batteries, promising technologies, are nonetheless part of the system of self-devouring growth. If car consumption continues to grow, the biofuel competition between food and energy, between forest and fuel, will follow. So too will the guns and money shoving Congolese miners into the earth in search of cobalt — until some day when that too is gone. And no doubt those batteries will return to Africa once their power ebbs — piled onto the trash heap of toxic waste.

Car/Cow

One often encounters livestock in Gaborone, as pasturage associated with surrounding villages has been taken over by the ever-growing capital. In 2007, while waiting for my pedicure appointment at a salon at Gaborone's upscale Riverwalk Mall, I stood at the railing on the veranda of the second floor with a small knot of onlookers, just one shop down from the Apache Spur Steakhouse where my daughter had recently celebrated her fourth birthday. Guards from the G4 Securicorps had chased a thief who ran from one of the shops as the store clerk yelled, "Legodu! LEGODU!" (Thief! THIEF!) A wiry young man in frayed green pants bolted through the car park and over an embankment when the security personnel unleashed their German shepherds. The crowd gasped that collective pause of both excitement and horror at the image of what was to happen when the dogs caught up with him. Suddenly a herd of cattle crossed the road and appeared in the foreground near the fleeing thief. The dogs pivoted and began herding the cattle, running in a circle around them as the man disappeared into the bush. "It's utter pandemonium," the older man next to me said in a completely deadpan voice, and then we all broke down laughing at his description of this quintessential Gaborone scene.

In January 2016 a leading daily newspaper in Botswana ran a story with a large full-color photo of two brown cows walking in the road in what appears to be an industrial neighborhood of Gaborone. The caption for the photo reads: "Wandering Eyesore: Herds of Cattle Are Increasingly Invading the Capital for Pasture."[84] The drought that drank the Gaborone Dam down only intensified the movement of thirsty cattle, who roamed in search of food and water. These were, presumably, the cows and oxen of smallholders who could ill afford their own boreholes— in other words cattle, not beef. Wandering the paved road, the cow, once the subject of poetry and aesthetic passion, had become an "eyesore."

Cars, like those parked at the Riverwalk Mall, had become the primary objects of desire—as diverse in their shapes and colors and features, their graceful movements, as cows of old. They were a form of pleasure inside which one could travel, perhaps while singing along to the radio. As anthropologist Deborah Durham writes about Botswana, "People *do* things with cars, beyond displaying status and self."[85] Navigating the road is necessary for work, work seeking, and socializing. Those who have walked for miles or waited in the hot sun, biting wind, or driving rain to pay for the privilege of cramming into a combi or bus have dreamed of the luxury of the private car. You could haul water canisters from the tap or the bowsing truck in your car's open trunk, and plastic bags of beef and other groceries from the supermarket. And cars are the quintessential status symbol, all the more so in a country whose wealthy business and political elite, like the elite everywhere it seems, do enjoy the leather interior of a Mercedes Benz.

Plenty of people are carless in Botswana. Even among the employed, there are many who sacrifice meals to afford combi fare to and from their low-wage jobs, especially at the end of the month as they await their next paycheck. And despite all efforts, unemployment has remained a significant problem for decades. That said, there are also plenty of cars. What is the road without the car? In fact, Botswana enjoys what is considered to be among the highest number of motor vehicles per capita in the developing world.[86]

In the mid-1990s used cars from Japan began to appear for sale here and there in Botswana. At first some people were suspicious of these vehicles, dubbing them "Fong Kong" as they did the imitation electronics and clothing that came from China, with the implication that these were lesser-quality goods. But it didn't take long for "Fong Kong" cars, which soon included some from Singapore as well, to find their market. Within a decade the cars had become something of a phenomenon. And by 2016 some 70 percent of all imported vehicles came from Japan, nearly all of them used.[87] Fong Kong cars were significantly cheaper than anything else on the market, and their availability, combined with a secondary market in consumer credit, fostered a steady rise in vehicle ownership.

In 2005 Botswana's car dealers, a powerful and well-connected business lobby, began complaining.[88] They cautioned that these cars may be of questionable quality and roadworthiness, that odometers or other records might have been falsified, and that local garages did not stock replacement parts for many of the models, making repairs difficult and expensive. They cautioned that these cars might cause their businesses to fold.[89] Eventually, Fong Kong cars were blamed for escalating traffic congestion and pollution as well.[90]

In return, resentment toward the dealers and others making these critiques was understandably high. As one new car owner put it, "Why should the poor people's property be the one to be blamed for everything every time?"[91] For many who were now finally acquiring their very own car, these were the sorts of complaints one hears from the elite when finally the common people have a turn—sort of like bemoaning the day-trippers on Nantucket from the veranda of one's beachfront home.[92] This was a sentiment shared for some time by the government, which, despite pressure from the dealers, some of whom were major donors to the ruling party, allowed the Fong Kong cars in. The Botswana ambassador to Japan, Oscar Motswagae, was quoted as saying that President Festus Mogae "felt that Batswana should be given an opportunity to own cars."[93] But by 2016, some eight years after Mogae stepped down, the new transport minister, formerly the environment minister and himself a trained auto-mechanic and engineer, threatened to cut off the supply of these imports. Facebook lit up with angry debate in which some lumped what they perceived as a government failure of transportation together with that of water supply.[94]

This of course gets us into the heart of one of the most challenging aspects of self-devouring growth. As soon as the poor finally get their turn, everyone cries foul. The rich, consuming at a rate far greater than any poor person can hope to match, have dirtied the rains, polluted the sea and air, and digested great swaths of life like the sperm whale, the bison, and the coal-bearing mountain until they wobbled on the edge of oblivion, only to smugly pronounce that some things shouldn't be consumed after all (as they go on consuming). The self-devouring nature of Fong Kong cars reveals yet another layer of this relationship. In order to see this, we have to follow the cars back to Japan.

Japan exports well over a million used cars per year.[95] Japanese drivers own over 76 million passenger cars, SUVs, and pickup trucks. But Japanese law dictates a regime of extremely costly and rigorous inspections and certification for all vehicles after three years on the road, which must then be repeated every other year. These regulations help to maintain high standards for vehicle emissions and for roadworthiness, thereby helping to moderate pollution and to minimize the breakdowns that bring traffic to a halt. This system is predicated on a consumption cycle encouraging drivers to replace older cars with new ones regularly, and given the onerous and expensive inspection regime it has all but negated any domestic market for used cars.

But then what is Japan to do with their used vehicles if they can't be sold domestically? Many cars are scrapped and dismantled so that parts can be reused or recycled. Strict regulations mandate the scrapping process — for example, fluorocarbons from air-conditioning systems need to be recovered and processed separately, as do airbags. The unsalvageable portion of the car is shredded and placed in a landfill. That portion previously accounted for some 20–25 percent of the total weight of the car, but this is changing as manufacturers seek to make more of the car recyclable.[96] But with landfill space at a premium, exporting used cars is nonetheless a necessary and profitable part of Japanese car consumption. And we all know the mantra that reuse is better than recycling. But if we then follow the Fong Kong onward, we might ask: better for whom?

This gray market stretches onto multiple continents. A decade before Botswana's car dealers began complaining to the government about the potential collapse of their businesses, New Zealand's dealers and assemblers were doing so in the face of Japanese used-car imports.[97] By 2003 Russian and American carmakers were also finding their business in Russia imperiled as the flood of cheap used Japanese cars was revolutionizing Russian car ownership.[98] With their right-sided steering wheels, Japanese used cars are particularly appealing in places like Botswana, to which Britain bequeathed the system of driving on the left-hand side of the road. The United States is also a major exporter of used cars, but theirs tend to go to Mexico and Central America.

As the cars are loaded into containers, headed overseas on enormous ships belching the exhaust of particularly sulfur-laden bunker fuel, Japan exports its pollution and traffic problems. While South Africa, in a bid to protect its own car-making industry, does not allow importation of used Japanese cars (though the port of Durban is the major transit center for Fong Kong cars in the southern Africa region), in Kenya 99 percent of imported cars are used.[99] Namibia and Botswana both recently introduced legislation that bans imports of vehicles older than five years, but they are currently in the minority. The average age of vehicles imported to Uganda is 16.5 years.[100] In the global south the cars have found a home without the same rigorous emissions and roadworthiness inspection regimes. In order to keep Kyoto's traffic flowing, these cars will break down on Nairobi's already overcrowded roads. For Japan's drivers to conserve with ever more fuel-efficient models, Myanmar's drivers will consume more petrol and produce more exhaust. Eventually, when they have finally run their course, they will be scrapped in a Pakistani rather than a Japanese landfill, most likely without having had their fluorocarbons drained. While Osaka's schoolchildren will have a clear view across their city, Onitsha's will cough up particulate as they squint through the smog. And yet this is probably not something most Japanese car owners will ever even realize.

If the toxic, indeed carcinogenic, nature of automobility is something we tacitly accept without question, carcinogenic refusal brought the cycle of self-consuming growth briefly into visibility, beginning in 2011. At that time, radioactive second-hand cars and car parts began showing up at ports and dealerships in the aftermath of the Fukushima nuclear disaster. Cars that were parked within the evacuation zone were apparently resold into the export market by "unscrupulous used car dealers" and by criminal syndicates who disguised the vehicles' origins.[101] Meanwhile, rain and wheels carried radiation to other vehicles farther afield, which also found their way into Japanese ports bound for the international trade.[102] These cars were tucked into a larger shipment to Chile in 2011, sparking protests by Chilean dockworkers. In reply, the Chilean nuclear commission declared their level of radioactivity safe for entry after being hosed down while still aboard ship so that any radiation would be "contained inside the ship."[103] This was only the beginning. Revealing the incredible and carcinogenic cynicism of the exporters, radioactive goods were sent around the globe for several years hence.

Contaminated cars subsequently appeared in Ugandan dealerships. Several were impounded in a container at the port of Mombasa in January 2013 and held for over a year, at great cost to the importer, before eventually being sent back to Japan. Kenya had hired a Japanese firm to inspect vehicles before they left Japan, only to find later that the company failed to do its job properly.[104] Meanwhile, in Kyrgyzstan seventy cars sat nervously impounded in Bishkent as officials tried to figure out what to do with them. Though Kyrgyzstan had already sent back several previous shipments of irradiated used cars to Japan through a mutual agreement with the Japanese government, by 2014 both Japan and China (through which, apparently they had been routed and cleared) refused to accept them.[105] Russia blocked several shipments of used cars from entering, including one of 132 used cars arriving at Vladivostok in 2014. Guyana, which lacks a Geiger counter, was fortunate that Jamaican officials detected the ionizing radiation emanating from a 40-foot container of vehicle parts en route to Guyana, which they subsequently seized and quarantined.[106] That these carcinogenic cars should arrive in places with no Geiger counters and limited oncology services is a diorama of the public health implications of self-devouring growth.

The car is both pleasure and millstone. Those who manage to acquire their own car may soon find themselves back on foot or worse. Even at half the price of a South African–made model, a Fong Kong car is still a very expensive machine. Just like in the United States, where working-class and poor people must have cars but cannot afford them, in Botswana the car loan closed the gap. Before 2006 banks didn't offer car loans for imported used cars, but with Fong Kong cars in high demand, they began financing them in great numbers.

If not a car loan, many buyers simply used a personal loan. A credit economy that had been growing steadily since the early 1990s was already underlying the boom in consumption in Botswana—refrigerators to store the beef, new homes made of aggregate, or upgrades to old ones like the introduction of indoor plumbing, could all be accessed by loans. In 2005 the Bank of Botswana reported that commercial banks made loans of 5.3 billion pula (roughly USD 1 billion) for "household use."[107] At that time commercial banks were pushing personal loans, popularly called *No Mathata*, Setswana for "no problem," for amounts between 12,000 and 75,000 pula. These amounts have been extended since then, with lower minimums and higher maximums at various banks. Depending on the prime rate, interest on the loan might reach as high as 30 percent. No Mathata loans were easy to access. Banks qualified borrowers who earn as little as 30,000 pula per annum. Along with the loan itself, borrowers were required to take out an insurance package in the event of premature death before the loan is paid.

Some people don't qualify for a No Mathata loan. Maybe they don't earn enough, or maybe they don't earn often. Maybe they already have borrowed so much that the banks won't extend them any more credit. For those lucky ones there are the *machonisa*—micro loan schemes, loan sharks really. Americans will recognize these as close cousins to our own predatory lenders—payday loans—offering loans for smaller amounts, at shorter terms, and higher interest rates and fees. By 2015 the IMF reported that *unsecured* household debt in Botswana had topped 15 billion pula (approximately USD 1.5 billion).[108] Meanwhile, the car must be fed its petrol and its oil. It must be repaired. Its tires or its CV joints must be replaced. Some people must drive their car to the pawnshop and leave it behind. Some find themselves back in the queue for the combi, with a portion of their pay garnished each month for that ailing cow of a car in their yard that refuses to move.

Debt becomes its own form of self-devouring growth. In Botswana a rising tide of suicides and murder-suicides has accompanied the tremendous stress of financialization and the growth of the credit industry.[109] So too in India, where the combination of global climate collapse, agribusiness, and debt has resulted in tens of thousands of suicides among farmers. And Botswana is far from alone in the region. As anthropologist Deborah James has so brilliantly examined, South Africans are highly leveraged, as credit-fueled consumerism blunted the political failures of postapartheid policies in the short term, producing new forms of abjection in the long term. This came to a head in 2012 at Lonmin's Marikana platinum mine near Rustenburg, close to the Botswana border. In August that year miners walked off the job and began a wildcat strike. Police, with the encouragement of management, opened fire using assault rifles. Dozens of miners were killed; even more were injured. Subsequent investigations revealed that many miners were highly leveraged, in the worst cases to the extent that their entire pay packet went to the machonisa each month.

As the road grows, it invents new places—suburbs, shopping malls, sprawl—spinning them out of aggregate, petroleum, and water. It draws forth energy—cobalt, ethanol, petroleum—whose violence is located elsewhere. Then one day the car is no longer a luxury, a cow, a dream. It has become a dead weight, a bloated carcass under which one buckles. Or perhaps a nightmare beast that flattened a child. In this regard, Botswana is slowly starting to resemble the United States. Anthropologist Catherine Lutz describes an American system of "compulsory consumption," whereby the car has become a fundamental economic necessity. In towns and cities determined by the road, a car is the sole means of mobility, and by virtue of this, cars have become objects that produce poverty and economic inequality,[110] all matter of carcinogenic exhaust. As Joni Mitchell's song suggests, at the conclusion of the road fairy tale there could be another haiku.

> Sand, water, oil for
> road might not have a happy
> ending after all.

4

Power and Possibility, or Did You Know Aesop Was Once a Slave?

And he said, A certain man had two sons.
−Luke 15:11

Intelligence is ongoing, individual adaptability.
Adaptations that an intelligent species may make
in a single generation, other species make over
many generations of selective breeding and
selective dying. Yet intelligence is demanding. If
it is misdirected by accident or by intent, it can
foster its own orgies of breeding and dying.
−Lauren Olamina, Earthseed: The Books of the Living

Lehatshe la rona le ile. le jewa ke baba botlhale.
−Sessio Man

BOTSWANA IS BEGINNING A NEW growth spurt; she's primed to metabolize another layer of her ancient bedrock. New roads may be coming, bearing trucks and heavy equipment. Already people who can afford it live behind walls topped with razor wire and broken glass; fortunate newcomers will join them. New wells are being sunk. Swimming pools have been dug and filled at the tourist lodges in the sand. The earth is rumbling. There's a boom and bust cycle brewing.

Cattle are taking over new parts of the delicate Kalahari. A new kind of drilling is under way, promising to do the same.[1]

After over a decade of rolling blackouts and scheduled power cuts, the Botswana government announced that power shortages were soon to be a thing of the past. In August 2017 a new license was issued to Tlou Energy, an Australian firm, whose executive director, Gabaake Gabaake, is the former permanent secretary of Botswana's Ministry of Minerals, Energy, and Water Resources. Tlou (Setswana for elephant) Energy received the first license of its kind for the development of coalbed methane extraction, to harvest a portion of the estimated 196 trillion cubic feet of methane contained in Botswana's massive coal deposits. Soon the country could hope to be free from dependence on importing power from South Africa and Zambia. Soon it would be free from dependence on costly foreign diesel. So clean-burning would this new gas be, and so vast are the deposits, that it was touted in the press alongside the tiny solar plant already in use as part of a single strategy for "clean" and "sustainable" energy. Within weeks of the government announcement, Tlou Energy shares were up by 12.3 percent.

The blackouts had been a problem. Traffic lights would go out, adding treachery and chaos to urban roads. Children in electrified homes were forced to schedule their study time around the load shedding. I remember arriving at the hospital one day and a doctor telling me that the previous night the backup generator had failed to kick in during a power cut. Flashlights appeared in the operating theater as a mechanic was sent out back to coax the generator to life. I myself have done more than my fair bit of whining amid the oppressive heat while waiting for the return of the electricity to churn the blades in my electric fan. Californians who remember the electricity crisis of the early 2000s will sympathize with the frustration of Batswana for whom power cuts had become an expected part of life. For most of the past decade, Botswana's electricity demands were more than double its capacity. People complained. They wanted power.

In April 2017 a rare but powerful 6.5 magnitude earthquake shook central Botswana from deep inside her rock. People as far away as Swaziland felt the ground tremble. Two days later another tremor came. Scientists soon established that the quake was not the result of human activity. But by this point public suspicion across the region had already drawn attention to the new companies undertaking gas extraction in the vast reaches of Botswana's interior.[2]

News of the drilling had trickled out over the preceding few years, beginning with the release of a film exposé and an article in the *Guardian* newspaper in 2013. The filmmakers discovered that for over a decade Botswana had been issuing prospecting licenses for shale gas (fracking) and coalbed methane (CBM) extraction in the Central Kalahari Game Reserve (CKGR), the second biggest wildlife refuge on earth. In its response to the revelation, the government split hairs. This was "drilling" not "fracking." Some "may view" the explosives-driven subsurface fracturing "as a type of fracking." These were prospecting licenses, not actual mining contracts. But amid the parsing of language and assurances that any move from prospecting to mining would include "environmental clearances," the ox was already out of the kraal as it were.[3]

Like hydraulic fracturing (fracking), CBM extraction requires vast quantities of water. As the U.S. Environmental Protection Agency explained in its 2010 study of CBM sites in the United States, once discharged, this water can be highly saline.[4] It cannot simply be disposed onto the veld or it will kill the grasses and plants on which the whole ecosystem depends. Surface discharge water has also been found to contain metals and other pollutants that need to be removed lest they contaminate the groundwater.[5] In some cases, it seems that methane can migrate from the drilling site and contaminate water supplies. Meanwhile, the pumping of vast quantities of water from the aquifer necessary for the extraction process threatens to sink the water table yet farther in Botswana's parched interior. Like fracking, CBM extraction also requires vast quantities of sand.[6] Just as beef has already pitted food against water in this arid country, and ethanol competes with food in Zimbabwe, the story continues apace. An abundance of power may someday mean a shortage of water and sand.

The filmmakers had documented evidence of drilling, and

interviewed drillers who had fracking equipment and referred to their work as such.[7] It soon became clear that prospecting licenses had been issued for half of the vast CKGR, as well as an area covering more than half of Botswana's side of the Kgalagadi Transfrontier Park (KTP), which straddles the Botswana–South Africa border and forms part of a vital corridor for seasonal wildlife migration—an animal road, if you will. Prospecting licenses were also in place for areas within Chobe National Park, home to the largest elephant population on earth, and in areas near the salt pans, another wildlife migration corridor through which the elephants and others transit.[8] Neither park managers nor leaders of the San communities whose ancestral homelands encompass the Kalahari had been consulted.[9]

This gas prospecting is mainly in the dry west and center of the country, home to San and Kgalagadi minority groups among others. In this region poverty is concentrated and palpable. The western minority groups who comprise much of Botswana's underclass have struggled for decades for political recognition and water rights from a nation that, perceiving them as relics of a primitive past, sought to "develop" them through mass relocations and sedentarization.[10]

In recent years, San communities have been pushed off their land and sometimes loaded onto cattle trucks in the name of wildlife conservation. They've had their water supply cut before being resettled into camps in the name of their own development and well-being. Meanwhile, new diamond mines, and now shale and CBM fields, were being developed in their ancestral home. Indigenous activists had successfully sued the government of Botswana, in the nation's longest-running court case, over their rights to reside in the CKGR. Yet over time, the withholding of water by the state and other forms of attrition have in effect nullified these rights, part of the emerging political dispensation in Botswana that political scientist Kenneth Good has termed "authoritarian liberalism."[11] No matter their protests, those of conservationists, and of others who are deeply concerned about the potential effects of fracking and CBM extraction. This new "clean fuel" industry is at hand. Though as anthropologist Pierre du Plessis suggests, the very sand of the Kalahari may take matters into its own hands.[12]

British colonialism rendered Botswana a migrant labor reserve for South African industry, leaving deep impoverishment in its wake. As the new nation sought to outgrow that poverty, public goods have been acknowledged as a "rightful share" of common wealth.[13] Roads, telecommunications, health care, electricity, water, education, peace, nature preserves—all this and more has been built. It *is* a miracle. Botswana is a testament to the tremendous abilities of her people. Were the story to end there, it would not be a parable, because the lesson would be clear. But sadly, it does not. Instead, we come to learn that our protagonist, Botswana, may soon be in peril. She is gnawing off her own leg to get out of a trap of her own making. We all are.

In the fall of 2017 I sat watching reports on television of the devastating aftermath of Hurricane Harvey in Texas. A reporter stood outside an oil refinery in Port Arthur and marveled at the destruction of homes, the precarious and overwhelming situation in which the working poor residents of this city found themselves. But he did not turn around and look at the refinery itself. He did not say that this refinery was part of a global petrochemical network that helped foster changes in our climate. Nor did he note that this refinery was carcinogenic to those who lived and worked in its shadow and that it bled chemicals like carbon monoxide, or that benzene washed into the flood waters.[14] He didn't note that he had driven to this scene in a gasoline-powered van, nor look into the camera and say to me in the comfort of my living room that I too likely used the fuel, the chemicals produced in this city. His report was a spectacle—not a parable like this one. In order to apprehend and face the enormity of our predicament, we must stop cleaving our dreams and nightmares asunder—such that the side effects and desired effects of consumption-driven growth are considered in isolation from one another.

Food, water, movement. All are necessary to human and other vital forms of life. All are complex relationships rather than resources that exist in isolation. Recognizing as much is necessary to understanding the difference between growth that is healthy and growth that is self-devouring. The animated ecology is not a bank from which humans compete to extract. It is a living manifestation of myriad, ongoing historical relationships. It is a future world we create every day in the present. It is a future world that depends on collective self-agreement to maintain. What happens if we eviscerate the animated ecology? What use are our ancestors in such a world? What use will we be when we become those ancestors?

The response to this cancer metastasizing in our midst cannot be to declare futility and walk away. Our heroine requires tending, though healing her animated ecology may not come easy, and there are bound to be scars. In Botswana, the ethical temporality is the present continuous. When someone is sick or injured, those who care are expected to remain active in their responsibility to their patient. It is the regular performance of these commitments, the countless small acts of tending, that allow the potential for healing. As Lauren Olamina, the protagonist of the parables bestowed by the great prophetess of our time Octavia Butler, realized, "There is no end to what a living world will demand of you."

Olamina lived in a dystopic and violent near future. She worked in the present continuous to heal the animated ecology. She recognized self-devouring growth for what it was. As a hyper-empath and as a young black woman in California, she felt the violence it wrought particularly deeply. Out of its brutality and devastation she built a new community based on collective self-belief and forms of growth not predicated on ever-escalating consumption. You and I, reader, we would do well to heed the lessons of Octavia Butler's heroine. Perhaps we can grow new worlds that preempt that dystopic near future. As anthropologist Anna Tsing shows so brilliantly, in the compost of capitalist landscapes new kinds of growth are possible.[15] We intelligent creatures must grow a new world in the ash-bed of this one. The prodigal son returns and the fatted calf is slaughtered. He was lost, but now is found.

Self-devouring growth emerges out of processes of aggregation and future-making that harness the planet's lifeblood into distorted forms of expansion. These forms of growth lead to necrosis and ultimately to the death of the organism itself. This is a cancerous model—the mutation of the self, the dyad of consumption and growth out of control. Self-devouring growth expresses itself in localized forms of rot and pain. Poverty is its ground zero, but its metastatic spread spares no one. We address this problem in maldistributed technical processes of amelioration. We rightly celebrate individual victories, helpful technologies, small concessions of redistribution, but the larger patterns point elsewhere. And what are we to do? How is one to argue for less—even if self-devouring growth is the force that is undermining collective well-being? How is one to argue for less when not nearly everyone yet has enough? Let us ask ourselves—what would rainmaking on a planetary scale entail?

NOTES

PROLOGUE. A Planetary Parable

Epigraphs: Lauren Olamina, "Earthseed: The Books of the Living," in Octavia Butler, *Parable of the Sower* (New York: Grand Central Publishing, 1993); Serge Latouche, *Farewell to Growth* (Cambridge: Polity Press, 2009); George Monbiot, "The Gift of Death," *Guardian*, 11 December 2012.

1. Here are a few alternative versions of the parable I am reciting. There are too many to name them all here, including the significant literature from the Degrowth and Buen Vivir movements. Serge Latouche, *Farewell to Growth* (Cambridge: Polity Press, 2009); Wolfgang Sachs, ed., *The Development Dictionary*, 2nd ed. (London: Zed Books, 2010); Butler, *Parable of the Sower*; Octavia Butler, *Parable of the Talents* (New York: Grand Central Publishing, 1998); Andrew Ross, *Bird on Fire: Lessons from the World's Least Sustainable City* (New York: Oxford University Press, 2013); Elizabeth Povinelli, *Geontologies: A Requiem to Late Liberalism* (Durham, NC: Duke University Press, 2017); Bhrigupati Singh, *Poverty and the Quest for Life: Spiritual and Material Striving in Rural India* (Chicago: University of Chicago Press, 2015); *Water and Power: A California Heist* (film directed by Maria Zenovich, 2017); Ruth Wilson Gilmore, *Golden Gulag: Prisons, Surplus, Crisis, and Opposition in Globalizing California* (Berkeley: University of California Press, 2007); Eduardo Gudynas, "Buen Vivir: Today's Tomorrow," *Development* 54, no. 4 (2011): 441–447; Reviel Netz, *Barbed Wire: An Ecology of Modernity* (Middletown, CT: Wesleyan University Press, 2004); Ghassan Hage, *Is Racism an Environmental Threat?* (Cambridge: Polity Press, 2017); Giorgos Kallas, *Degrowth* (Newcastle upon Tyne: Agenda Publishing, 2018).

2. There is also a rich and important social science literature that takes up the failures of development and the violence (structural, cultural, intellectual, political, and economic) done in its name. These critiques are important, and this story does not contradict them but rather seeks to open a somewhat different narrative horizon. See, for example, Arturo Escobar,

Encountering Development: The Making and Unmaking of the Third World (Princeton, NJ: Princeton University Press, 2011); James Ferguson, *The Anti-politics Machine: Development, Depolitization, and Bureaucratic Power in Lesotho* (Minneapolis: University of Minnesota Press, 1994); James C. Scott, *Seeing Like the State: How Certain Schemes to Improve the Human Condition Have Failed* (New Haven, CT: Yale University Press, 1999); Tania Murray Li, *The Will to Improve: Governmentality, Development, and the Practice of Politics* (Durham, NC: Duke University Press, 2007); Akhil Gupta, *Red Tape: Bureaucracy, Structural Violence, and Poverty in India* (Durham, NC: Duke University Press, 2012); Timothy Mitchell, *Rule of Experts: Egypt, Technopolitics, Modernity* (Berkeley: University of California Press, 1992). This literature includes the fictionalized parable by Richard Rottenburg, *Far Fetched Facts: A Parable of Development Aid* (Cambridge: MIT Press, 2009).

3. Setswana is a Bantu language. Nouns are formed through a system of prefixes added to root words. For example, Tswana is a root and used as a generic referent to anything pertaining to a large ethnic group whose people reside mainly in Botswana and South Africa; Motswana is a single Tswana person or citizen of the modern nation of Botswana; Batswana are two or more Tswana people; Botswana is the collective noun for all things Tswana and hence the modern nation of Botswana; Setswana is the language and/or customs/knowledge of Tswana people.

4. I am grateful to Jennifer Wenzel for alerting me to this.

5. Amy-Jill Levine, *Short Stories by Jesus: The Enigmatic Parables of a Controversial Rabbi* (New York: Harper One, 2014). I am grateful to Zenia Kish for this reference. See also Kevin Mills, "Parables, A–Z," *The Yearbook of English Studies* 39, nos. 1–2 (2009): 194. I am grateful to Elaine Freedgood for this reference.

6. Abdi Ismail Samatar, *An African Miracle: State and Class Leadership and Colonial Legacy in Botswana Development* (Portsmouth, NH: Heinemann, 1999). This is not to say that there are not problems of corruption or power struggles or discrimination against ethnic minorities, etc., some of which will be shown in the tale that follows.

7. Both consumption of resources and production of waste currently occur at a higher rate than the planet can regenerate. Allesandro Galli, Thomas Wiedmannb, Ertug Ercinc, Doris Knoblauchd, Brad Ewinge, and Stefan Giljum, "Integrating Ecological, Carbon and Water Footprint into a 'Footprint Family' of Indicators: Definition and Role in Tracking Human Pressure on the Planet," *Ecological Indicators* 16 (2012): 100–111; Mathis Wackernagel, Larry Onisto, Patricia Bello, Alejandro Callejas Linares, Ina Susana López Falfán, Jesus Méndez García, Ana Isabel Suárez Guerrero, and Ma. Guadalupe Suárez Guerrero, "National Natural Capital Accounting with the Ecological Footprint Concept," *Ecological Economics* 29 (1999): 375–390.

8. See for example, James Fairhead and Melissa Leach, *Reframing Deforestation: Global Analyses and Local Realities: Studies in West Africa* (London: Routledge, 1998); Hannah Brown and Ann Kelly, "Material Proximities and Hot Spots: Toward an Anthropology of Viral Hemmorhagic Fevers," *Medical Anthropology Quarterly* 28(2), 2014: 280–303; Robert Wallace, Marius Gilbert, and Roderick Wallace, "Did Ebola Emerge in West Africa by a Policy-Driven Phase Change in Agroecology? Ebola's Social Context," *Environment and Planning A* 2014, 46 (2014): 2533–2542; Emmanual Kreike, *Deforestation and Reforestation in Namibia: The Global Consequences of Local Contradictions* (Leiden: Brill, 2010).

9. That includes an increase in days where the maximum temperature is projected to be between 39 and 51 degrees Celsius. Rebecca M. Garland, Mamopeli Matooane, Francois A. Engelbrecht, Mary-Jane M. Bopape, Willem A. Landman, Mogesh Naidoo, Jacobus van der Merwe, and Caradee Y. Wright, "Regional Projections of Extreme Apparent Temperature Days in Africa and the Related Potential Risk to Human Health," *International Journal of Environmental Research and Public Health* 12 (2015): 12577–12604

10. Naomi Klein, *The Shock Doctrine: The Rise of Disaster Capitalism* (New York: Picador, 2008).

11. Through the 1990s (when the first such data was systematically catalogued), Botswana was a net carbon sink, absorbing more greenhouse gases than the nation produced. *Botswana Initial National Communication to the United Nations Framework Convention on Climate Change* (Gaborone: Botswana Ministry of Works, Transport and Communications, 2001).

12. I am grateful to Kris Peterson for this phrasing.

13. S. Lochlann Jain, *Malignant: How Cancer Becomes Us* (Berkeley: University of California Press, 2014).

14. See Karen Bakker on the challenges of reducing the politics of water provision to public versus private. Karen Bakker, *Privatizing Water: Governance Failure and the World's Urban Water Crisis* (Ithaca, NY: Cornell University Press, 2010).

15. My point here is not to be glib about how the redistributive institutions of socialism offers a check on consumption. Rather I am saying that the beef that is part of the redistributive flow is coming from Botswana where it is having the opposite effect. This is something I am confident most Norwegian would never have cause to know. I am grateful to Libby Wood for helping me to think this through.

16. Vincanne Adams, *Markets of Sorrow, Labors of Faith: New Orleans in the Wake of Katrina* (Durham, NC: Duke University Press, 2013); Klein, *Shock Doctrine.*

17. *Elite Emissions: How the Homes of the Wealthiest New Yorkers Help Drive Climate Change* (Climate Works for All Coalition, 2015).

18. Latouche, *Farewell to Growth*, 23; see also Wackernagel et al., "National Nature Capital Accounting with the Ecological Footprint Concept"; V. Niccolucci, E. Tiezzi, F. M. Pulselli, and C. Capineri, "Biocapacity vs. Ecological Footprints of World Regions: A Geopolitical Interpretation," *Ecological Indicators* 16 (2012): 23–30.

19. Rob Nixon, *Slow Violence and the Environmentalism of the Poor* (Cambridge, MA: Harvard University Press, 2013).

20. Mexican author Gustavo Esteva explains that after Truman inaugurated the development paradigm in the late 1940s, foundational thinkers like Albert Lewis, the Caribbean economist and Nobel Laureate, understood development as synonymous with economic growth. In the ensuing decades, development proponents of a range of political persuasions from the radical left to the conservative right took up social issues in their own right (e.g., literacy, health). But the larger logic of development as measured by evolutionary stages of economic growth to which social developments were related or from which social developments were extensive has persisted. This relationship has taken various forms over time, and there have been key moments of disaggregation and dissent like in the 1970s. Gustavo Esteva, "Development," in Sachs, *The Development Dictionary*, 1–23.

21. Mitchell, *Rule of Experts*.

22. James Ferguson, *Give a Man a Fish: Reflections on the New Politics of Distribution* (Durham, NC: Duke University Press, 2015).

23. Brian Benza, "World Bank Warns Botswana," *Mmegi*, 10 July 2015, http://www.mmegi.bw/index.php?aid=52531&dir=2015%2Fjuly%2F10.

24. This critique is foundational to the Latin American literature on development cited above.

25. As Michel Foucault says, "No! I am not looking for an alternative; you can't find the solution of a problem in the solution of another problem raised at another moment by other people. You see, what I want to do is not the history of solutions, and that's the reason why I don't accept the word 'alternative.' I would like to do the genealogy of problems, of problématique. My point is not that everything is bad, but that everything is dangerous, which is not exactly the same as bad. If everything is dangerous, then we always have something to do. So my position leads not to apathy but to a hyper- and pessimistic activism." Michel Foucault, "On the Genealogy of Ethics," in *Michel Foucault: Beyond Structuralism and Hermeneutics*, ed. Hubert L. Dreyfus and Paul Rabinow (Chicago: University of Chicago Press, 1983), 231–232.

26. Jean Comaroff and John L. Comaroff, *Theory from the South: Or, How Euro-America Is Evolving toward Africa* (London: Routledge, 2012); Povinelli, *Geontologies*; Anna Lowenhaupt Tsing, *The Mushroom at the End of the World: On the Possibility of Life in Capitalist Ruins* (Princeton, NJ: Princeton University Press, 2015); Kristina Lyons, Juno Salazar Parrenas,

and Noah Tamarkin, "Critical Perspectives: Engagements with Decolonization and Decoloniality in and at the Interfaces of STS," *Catalyst: Feminism, Theory, Technoscience* 3, no. 1 (2017): 1–47.

27. Anthropologist Pierre du Plessis is working from another corner, and I am excited about the places where we meet. Pierre du Plessis, "Gathering the Kalahari: Tracks, Trails, and More-Than-Human Landscapes" (PhD dissertation, Aarhus University and University of California–Santa Cruz, joint program, 2018).

28. Paul Landau, *Popular Politics in the History of South Africa, 1400–1948* (Cambridge, MA: Cambridge University Press, 2013).

29. Landau, *Popular Politics*.

CHAPTER 1. Rainmaking and Other Forgotten Things

Epigraph: Bessie Head, *When Rain Clouds Gather* (New York: Simon and Schuster, 1969).

1. Felicity Barringer, "World's Aquifers Losing Replenishment Race, Scientists Say," *New York Times*, 25 June 2015, https://www.nytimes.com/2015/06/26/science/worlds-aquifers-losing-replenishment-race-researchers-say.html.

2. Department of Attorney General of Michigan, "Schuette Files Civil Suit against Veolia and LAN for Role in Flint Water Poisoning," https://www.michigan.gov/ag/0,4534,7-359-82917_78314-387198--,00.html.

3. Karen Bakker aptly observes that "water is, in some sense, a final frontier for capitalism." Karen Bakker, *Privatizing Water: Governance Failure and the World's Urban Water Crisis* (Ithaca, NY: Cornell University Press, 2010), 3.

4. Janet Roitman, *Anti-crisis* (Durham, NC: Duke University Press, 2013).

5. Veolia Water Technologies website, accessed December 2018, https://www.veoliawatertechnologies.com/en.

6. Veolia Water Technologies Botswana website, http://www.veoliawatertechnologies.co.za/about-us/organisation/veolia-water-technologies-botswana/. I am grateful to Victoria Koski-Karrell for drawing attention to this connection and for her keen engagement with an earlier draft of this chapter.

7. See, for example, Isaac Schapera, *Rainmaking Rites of Tswana Tribes* (Leiden: Afrika-Stuidecentrum, 1971); Paul Landau, "When Rain Falls: Rainmaking and Community in a Tswana Village c. 1870 to Recent Times," *International Journal of African Historical Studies* 26 (1993): 1–30; Jean Comaroff and John Comaroff, *Of Revelation and Revolution: Christianity, Colonialism, and Consciousness in South Africa*, vol. 1 (Chicago: University of Chicago Press, 1991); Julie Livingston, *Debility and the Moral Imagination in Botswana* (Bloomington: Indiana University Press, 2005).

8. In doing so I am following the lead of Timothy Choy, *Ecologies of Comparison: An Ethnography of Endangerment in Hong Kong* (Durham, NC: Duke University Press, 2011); Lesley Green, "Fracking, Oikos and Omics in the Karoo: Reimagining South Africa's Reparative Energy Politics," *Os Mil Nomes de Gaia*, September 2014, https://osmilnomesdeg aia.files.wordpress.com/2014/11/lesley-green.pdf; Jean Comaroff and John L. Comaroff, *Theory from the South: Or, How Euro-America Is Evolving toward Africa* (London: Routledge, 2012).

9. Dipesh Chakrabarty, "Climate and Capital: On Conjoined Histories," *Critical Inquiry* 41 (Autumn 2014): 1–23; Isabelle Stengers, *In Catastrophic Times: Resisting the Coming Barbarism* (London: Open Humanities Press, 2015); Naomi Oreskes and Erik M. Conway, *The Collapse of Western Civilization: A View from the Future* (New York: Columbia University Press, 2014).

10. Botswana is by no means the only site where one might look for possibilities. The world (past and present) is full of ideas, technologies, and forms of governance that were undermined, set aside, denigrated by the same forces of Euro-American industrialization and empire in which we find the seeds of our current water crisis. See, for example, Green, "Fracking, Oikos and Omics in the Karoo"; Noelani Goodyear-Ka'opua, introduction to *A Nation Rising: Hawaiian Movements for Life, Land, and Sovereignty*, ed. Noelani Goodyear-Kaʻōpua, Ikaika Hussey, and Erin Kahunawaikaʻala Wright (Durham, NC: Duke University Press, 2014), 1–34; Elizabeth A. Povinelli, *Geontologies: A Requiem to Late Liberalism* (Durham, NC: Duke University Press, 2016).

11. Cloud seeding is not the same as rainmaking.

12. Toby Jones, *Desert Kingdom: How Oil and Water Forged Modern Saudi Arabia* (Cambridge, MA: Harvard University Press, 2010).

13. On wealth in people, see Jane Guyer and Samuel M. Eno Belinga, "Wealth in People as Wealth in Knowledge: Accumulation and Composition in Equatorial Africa," *Journal of African History* 36, no. 1 (1995): 91–120.

14. See, for example, Steven Feierman, *Peasant Intellectuals: Anthropology and History in Tanzania* (Madison: University of Wisconsin Press, 1990); Landau, "When Rain Falls"; Todd Sanders, *Beyond Bodies: Rain-Making and Sense-Making in Tanzania* (Toronto: University of Toronto Press, 2008); Eileen Krige, *The Realm of a Rain Queen: A Study of the Patterns of Lovedu Society* (London: Routledge, 1943); Elizabeth Colson, "Rain-Shrines of the Plateau Tonga of Northern Rhodesia," *Africa* 18 (1948): 272–283.

15. The above synthesis is drawn from Schapera, *Rainmaking Rites of Tswana Tribes*; Landau, "When Rain Falls"; Julie Livingston, *Debility and the Moral Imagination in Botswana* (Bloomington: Indiana University Press, 2005), chapter 2.

16. "Bakgatla Affairs: Domestic Relations between Isang's Family and

Chief Molefi's Family," *Confidential District Commissioner's Report* (1934), Botswana National Archives, S.305/19.

17. Schapera, *Rainmaking Rites of Tswana Tribes*, 20.

18. Schapera, *Rainmaking Rites of Tswana Tribes*, 20.

19. See https://www.facebook.com/permalink.php?story_fbid=68457 5591625102&id=148228411926492.

20. Mtokozisi Dube, "President Khama Has Rainmaking Powers," *Africa Review* 17 (January 2013), http://www.africareview.com/News/Pr esident-Khama-has-rainmaking-powers-/-/979180/1668048/-/uqniktz /-/index.html.

21. Republic of Botswana Government Portal, 21 June 2013, https:// www.facebook.com/BotswanaGovernment/posts/southern-dams-at -critical-levelgaborone-dam-the-only-water-oasis-for-most-people/4724 25716173425/.

22. Tshepo Mongwa, "Khama Asks for Prayers," *Botswana Daily News*, 29 August 2013, http://www.dailynews.gov.bw/news-details.php?nid=5324.

23. Botswana is not the only technocratic nation organizing prayers for rain in the face of drought. In 2017 the Israeli minister of agriculture did the same. Zafrir Renat, "Israeli Agriculture Minister's Solution to Drought: Mass Western Wall Prayers for Rain," *Haaretz*, 24 December 2017, https:// www.haaretz.com/israel-news/israeli-minister-s-solution-to-drought -mass-prayers-for-rain-1.5629432. I am grateful to Andrew Ross for this reference.

24. "Botswana Churches Not Properly Consulted in Gaborone Dam Prayers," GABZ-FM, 9 September 2013, 17:00, http://www.gabzfm.com /botswana-churches-not-properly-consulted-gaborone-dam-prayers.

25. John Regonamanye, "Prayer for Rain," *Sunday Standard*, 22 September 2013, http://www.sundaystandard.info/article.php?NewsID=18002& GroupID=2.

26. The Molatedi dam, located in Zeerust, South Africa, is on the Marico River, which forms part of the border between South Africa and Botswana. By an agreement made in 1988, a portion of the dam water is piped to Botswana, supplying over 4 million liters a day to Gaborone. But this dam was also drying up; as of September 2015 it was at 8.4 percent of capacity and the terms of the water-sharing arrangement were scheduled to be renegotiated. Mbongeni Mguni, "SA to Cut Off Water Supply," *Mmegi*, 22 September 2015, http://www.mmegi.bw/index.php?aid=54310 &dir=2015%2Fseptember%2F22#sthash.Wj9XLEeB.dpuf.

27. Baboki Kayawe, "Water Crisis Cripples Marina Operations," *Mmegi*, 2 September 2015, http://www.mmegi.bw/index.php?aid=53799&dir= 2015/september/02.

28. Phillimon Mmeso, "Cheap Politics or Genuine March?," *Patriot on Sunday*, 7 September 2015, http://www.thepatriot.co.bw/news/item/14 01-cheap-politics-or-genuine-march.html. Earlier rhetoric also called for investment in solar energy.

29. Bame Piet, "UDC Just Being Childish — Mokaila," *Mmegi*, 4 September 2015, http://www.mmegi.bw/index.php?aid=53877&dir=2015%2Fseptember%2F04. See also this commentary by an unnamed analyst, "Lack of Rain Is Not a Political Problem," *Monitor*, 7 September 2015, http://www.mmegi.bw/index.php?aid=53905&dir=2015%2Fseptember%2F07, and the opposing view: Michael Dingake, "Are Protest Demonstrations Childish?," *Mmegi*, 8 September 2015, http://www.mmegi.bw/index.php?aid=53947&dir=2015/september/08.

30. Mmeso, "Cheap Politics or Genuine March?"

31. In Africa this began with the Kariba Dam (completed in 1958) and continued with the Aswan High (Egypt), Volta (Ghana), Kainji (Nigeria), and others.

32. This is the process João Biehl has called the "pharmaceuticalization of public health." See João Biehl, "Pharmaceuticalization: AIDS Treatment and Global Health Politics," *Anthropological Quarterly* 80, no. 4 (2007): 1083–1126.

33. Peter Redfield, "Fluid Technologies: The Bush Pump, the Life Straw, and Microworlds of Humanitarian Design," *Social Studies of Science* 46, no. 2 (2016): 159–183.

34. Anne-Emanuelle Birn, Yogan Pillay, and Timothy Holtz, *Textbook of International Health: Global Health in a Dynamic World*, 3rd ed. (New York: Oxford University Press, 2009), 498.

35. See Patrick Bond, "Water, Health, and the Commodification Debate," *Review of Radical Political Economy* 42 (2010): 445–464.

36. IMF *Country Report No. 14/204: Botswana*, July 2014, 5, http://www.imf.org/external/pubs/ft/scr/2014/cr14204.pdf.

37. The Botswana government has noted that while 66 percent of potable water in the country comes from groundwater, "groundwater recharge is very limited, thus making the resource finite and non-renewable." Government of Botswana, *Botswana Water Statistics* (Gaborone: Central Statistics Office, 2009), 15.

38. Linda Qiu, "Botswana: Diamond Hopes, Diamond Blues," *Huffington Post*, 20 August 2013, http://pulitzercenter.org/reporting/africa-botswana-mochudi-water-boreholes-drills-diamond-minerals-mine-poverty-unhealthy-untreated-government-cattle-gaborone-dam-thirst-hydraulic-commerical-farmers.

39. Pini Bothoko, "Botswana's Water Is Bad — BOBS," *Mmegi*, 22 June 2015, http://www.mmegi.bw/index.php?aid=52088&dir=2015%2Fjune%2F22. In September 2015 an outbreak of 168 cases of diarrheal disease in Ramotswa, particularly acute among children under five, was suspected to be linked to the ongoing water crisis. Baboki Kayawe, "Of Diarrhea, Health and the Water Crisis," *Mmegi*, 4 September 2015, http://www.mmegi.bw/index.php?aid=53867&dir=2015/september/04.

40. William G. Moseley, "Africa's Future? Botswana's Growth with

Hunger," *Al Jazeera English*, 7 May 2012, https://www.aljazeera.com/in depth/opinion/2012/05/201254115536921635.html.

41. James Ferguson, "The Bovine Mystique: Power, Property, and Livestock in Rural Lesotho," *Man*, n.s., 20 (1985): 647–674.

42. Martin Whiteside, *Living Farms: Encouraging Sustainable Smallholders in Southern Africa* (Abingdon, UK: Earthscan, 2013), 17; Peter P. Zhou, Tichakunda Simbini, Gorata Ramokgotlwane, Timothy S. Thomas, Sepo Hachigonta, and Lindiwe Majele Sibanda, "Botswana," in *Southern African Agriculture and Climate Change: A Comprehensive Analysis*, ed. Sepo Hachigonta, Gerald C. Nelson, Timothy S. Thomas, and Lindiwe M. Sibanda (Washington, DC: International Food Policy Research Institute, 2013), http://www.ifpri.org/sites/default/files/publications/rr 179ch03.pdf.

43. Peter P. Zhou, Tichakunda Simbini, Gorata Ramokgotlwane, Sepo Hachigonta, Lindiwe Sibanda, and Timothy S. Thomas, "Botswana," in Southern African Agriculture and Climate Change: A Comprehensive Analysis" (Washington, DC: International Food Policy Research Institute, 2013), http://cdm15738.contentdm.oclc.org/utils/getfile/collection /p15738coll2/id/127287/filename/127498.pdf.

44. Innocent Selathlwa, "Heatwave 'Silently' Claims Lives," *Mmegi*, 8 January 2016, http://www.mmegi.bw/index.php?aid=56812&dir=2016 %2Fjanuary%2F08.

45. Schapera, *Rainmaking Rites of Tswana Tribes*, 54–59.

46. Sherine Hamdy and I developed this term together. I am, as always, grateful to her.

47. Mansur Mirovalev, "Uzbekistan: A Dying Sea, Mafia Rule, and Toxic Fish," *Al Jazeera*, 11 Jun 2015, http://www.aljazeera.com/indepth /features/2015/06/uzbekistan-dying-sea-mafia-rule-toxic-fish-1506 10102819386.html; "Impacts to Life in the Region," The Aral Sea Crisis, http://www.columbia.edu/~tmt2120/impacts%20to%20life%20in%20 the%20region.htm; Bakhodyr Muradov and Alisher Ilkhamov, *Working Paper: Uzbekistan's Cotton Sector: Financial Flows and Distribution of Resources* (New York: Open Society Eurasia Program, 2014), http://www .opensocietyfoundations.org/sites/default/files/uzbekistans-cotton -sector-20141021.pdf.

48. Some farmers paid meticulous attention to the timing of the rains and managed to reap significant harvests in May 2016. Jackie Solway, personal communication. Tsaone Basimanebotlhe and Mbongeni Mguni, "Floods Cripple Ramotswa," *Mmegi*, 16 March 2016, http://www.mmegi .bw/index.php?aid=58608&dir=2016/march/16; "Botswana: Floods Took Nation by Surprise — Makgalemele," *Botswana Daily News*, 29 March 2016.

49. Mbongeni Mguni, "Go and Plough, Radithupa Urges Doubting Thomases," *Mmegi*, 18 November 2016, http://www.mmegi.bw/index.php ?aid=64738&dir=2016/november/18.

50. "Rains Cause Havoc in Moshupa," *Botswana Daily News*, 8 January 2017; "Moshupa Re-builds as Flood Waters Recede," *Botswana Daily News*, 10 January 2017.

51. Goitsemodimo Kaelo, "'Stubborn' Gaborone Dam Gains Steadily," *Mmegi*, 31 January 2017, http://www.mmegi.bw/index.php?aid=66245 &dir=2017/january/31.

52. Boingotlo Seitshiro, "Floods in the South," *Mmegi*, 21 February 2017, http://www.mmegi.bw/index.php?aid=66799&dir=2017/february/21.

53. Nnasaretha Kgamanyane, "Heavy Rains Flood Southern Botswana," *Mmegi*, 22 February 2017, http://www.mmegi.bw/index.php?aid=66836 &dir=2017/february/22.

54. Tsaone Basimanebotlhe, "Floods: Patients, Corpses Moved and Schools Closed," *Mmegi*, 23 February 2017, http://www.mmegi.bw/index .php?aid=66868&dir=2017/february/23.

55. Lebogang Mosikare, "Floods Leave Trail of Destruction in Nata-Gweta," *Mmegi*, 3 March 2017, http://www.mmegi.bw/index.php?aid=67 115&dir=2017/march/03.

56. "President Khama, Together with Members of the Cabinet to Hold Prayers Near Gaborone Dam This Sunday," *Botswana Guardian*, 27 February 2017, http://www.botswanaguardian.co.bw/news/item/2380-presi dent-khama-together-with-members-of-the-cabinet-to-hold-prayers -near-gaborone-dam-this-sunday.html.

CHAPTER 2. In the Time of Beef

1. Pauline Peters, *Dividing the Commons: Politics, Policy, and Culture in Botswana* (Charlottesville: University of Virginia Press, 1994).

2. On that dynamic tension, see Debbie Durham, "Soliciting Gifts and Negotiating Agency: The Spirit of Asking in Botswana," *Journal of the Royal Anthropological Institute* 1, no. 1 (1995): 111–128.

3. These two poems were collected by Van der Merwe and published in *Bantu Studies* in 1941 and subsequently reproduced by anthropologist Hoyt Alverson in *Mind in the Heart of Darkness: Value and Self-Identity among the Tswana of Southern Africa* (New Haven, CT: Yale University Press, 1978).

4. Alverson, *Mind in the Heart of Darkness*, 127.

5. Jean Comaroff and John Comaroff, "Goodly Beasts, Beastly Goods," *American Ethnologist* 17, no. 2 (1990): 197.

6. Isaac Schapera, *The Tswana* (1953; London: International Africa Institute, 1979), 226.

7. Alverson, *Mind in the Heart of Darkness*, 124.

8. Comaroff and Comaroff, "Goodly Beasts," 206.

9. Jacqueline Solway, "Taking Stock in the Kalahari: Accumulation and Resistance on the Southern African Periphery," *Journal of Southern African Studies* 24, no. 2 (1998): 425–441.

10. Isaac Schapera and John L. Comaroff, *The Tswana*, rev. ed. (London: Keegan Paul, 1991), 17.

11. Abdi Ismail Samatar, *An African Miracle: State and Class Leadership and Legacy in Botswana Development* (Portsmouth, NH: Heinemann, 1999), 113. See also changes in breeding over the twentieth century: L. L. Lethola, N. G. Buck, and D. E. Light, "Beef Cattle Breeding in Botswana," *Botswana Notes and Records* 15, no. 1083 (1983): 39–47.

12. Alverson, *Mind in the Heart of Darkness*, 158.

13. Alverson, *Mind in the Heart of Darkness*, 128.

14. As Ornulf Gulbrandsen argues, the presence of the beef industry helped pave the way for diamonds. Gulbrandsen, *The State and the Social: State Formation in Botswana and Its Precolonial and Colonial Genealogies* (New York: Berghahn Books, 2012).

15. Samatar, *An African Miracle*, 116.

16. Balefi Tsie, *The Political Economy of Botswana in SADCC* (Harare: Sapes Books, 1995), 240–241.

17. The Tribal Lands Grazing Policy being the most significant, perhaps.

18. Anton Van Engelen, Patrick Malope, John Keyser, and David Neven, *Botswana Agrifood Value Chain Project: Beef Value Chain Study* (Rome and Gaborone: UN FAO and Botswana Ministry of Agriculture, 2013), 58.

19. I am grateful to Rachel Cypher for pointing this out to me.

20. "FMD Episode V: The Abattoir Strikes Back," posted 9 July 2011, https://bengolas.wordpress.com/2011/07/09/fmd-episode-v-the-abattoir-strikes-back/. This same man would go on in a later post to criticize the culture of neglect of animals among some in Botswana—by hired hands. Ironic, as he did not know that the system in which he labored was part of the economy that cleaved the apotheosis of the cow from the beef industry.

21. I am grateful to Charlie Piot for this idea and turn of phrase.

22. I am grateful to Jackie Soloway for this observation.

23. Beginning with a vaccine against foot-and-mouth, they have expanded capacity to produce vaccines against contagious bovine pleuropneumonia, *peste des petits ruminants*, anthrax, and blackquarter. According to the BVI website, they now supply millions of doses annually to more than fifteen sub-Saharan countries.

24. Pule Phoofolo, "Epidemics and Revolutions: The Rinderpest Epidemic in Late Nineteenth-Century Southern Africa," *Past and Present* 138, no. 1 (1993): 125.

25. Phoofolo, "Epidemics and Revolutions," 132.

26. J. B. Peires, *The Dead Will Arise: Nonqgawuse and the Great Xhosa Cattle-Killing Movement of 1856–7* (Bloomington: Indiana University Press, 1989).

27. "10,000 Cattle to Be Burnt," *Mmegi*, 6 May 2011, http://www.mmegi.bw/index.php?sid=1&aid=672&dir=2011/May/Friday6.

28. Ryder Gabathuse, "FMD Chaos!," *Mmegi*, 5 May 2011, http://www

.mmegi.bw/index.php?sid=1&aid=605&dir=2011%2FMay%2FThursday5&fb_comment_id=10150181621800340_16851328.

29. Keabetswe Newel, "Matsiloje Farmers Confront Minister over FMD Outbreak," *Mmegi*, 9 May 2011, http://www.mmegi.bw/index.php?sid=1&aid=706&dir=2011/May/Monday9/.

30. Mbongeni Mguni, "BMC Hits Record Slaughter Figures," *Mmegi*, 27 January 2011, http://www.mmegi.bw/index.php?sid=4&aid=460&dir=2011/January/Thursday27.

31. Frederick Kebadiretse, "60,000 Live Cattle to Be Exported to Zim," *Mmegi*, 28 October 2011, http://www.mmegi.bw/index.php?sid=4&aid=1059&dir=2011/October/Friday28.

32. "Debate Divides Botswana Parliament," *Citizen*, 26 May 2016, https://citizen.co.za/news/news-africa/1133585/debate-divides-botswana-parliament/.

33. Alverson, *Mind in the Heart of Darkness*, 128.

34. Jacqueline Solway, personal communication, 29 December 2017.

35. Most of the processed meat sold in domestic supermarkets is produced by Senn Foods, which is owned by Derek Brink, Botswana's largest cattle owner. Senn Foods has its own abattoir and sells directly into the domestic market, bypassing the BMC. Recently it has been lobbying for the liberalization of the beef market, which would allow it to export. Aubrey Lute, "Brink Pushes the BMC Styled Business Model," *Weekend Post*, 2 May 2017, http://www.weekendpost.co.bw/wp-news-details.php?nid=2731.

36. Michael Darkoh and Joseph Mbaiwa, "Globalization and the Livestock Industry in Botswana," *Singapore Journal of Tropical Geography* 23, no. 2 (2002): 160.

37. Van Engelen et al., *Botswana Agrifood Value Chain Project*, xi.

38. Lemogang Daniel Kwape, "Diet and Cardiovascular Disease Risk Factor in Botswana" (PhD dissertation, Public Health Nutrition Research Group, University of Aberdeen, 2012).

39. I am grateful to Laura Ann Twagira for coining the term the "taste of development." See Laura Ann Twagira, "Women and Gender at the Office du Niger (Mali): Technology, Environment, and Food ca. 1900–1985," PhD dissertation, History Department, Rutgers University, 2013.

40. Isaac Pinielo, "BMC Eyes Beef Exports to China," *Mmegi*, 8 May 2015, http://www.mmegi.bw/index.php?aid=51016&dir=2015/may/08.

41. Van Engelen et al., *Botswana Agrifood Value Chain Project*, 22.

42. Van Engelen et al., *Botswana Agrifood Value Chain Project*, 121.

43. Mompathi Tlhakane, "Kgatleng Meat Festival Fuses Beef, Entertainment," *Mmegi*, 13 April 2016, http://www.mmegi.bw/index.php?aid=59246&dir=2016/april/13.

44. Gobopamang Letamo, "The Prevalence of and Factors Associated with Overweight and Obesity in Botswana," *Journal of Biosocial Science* 43, no. 1 (2011): 75–84.

45. Lauren Berlant, "Slow Death (Sovereignty, Obesity, Lateral Agency)," *Critical Inquiry* 33, no. 4 (2007): 754–780.

46. Julie Livingston, "Pregnant Children and Half-Dead Adults: Modern Living and the Quickening Life-Cycle in Botswana," *Bulletin of the History of Medicine* 77, no. 1 (2003): 133–162.

47. WHO Fact Sheet, *Obesity and Overweight*, June 2016, http://www.who.int/mediacentre/factsheets/fs311/en/.

48. Lauren Berlant, "Slow Death (Sovereignty, Obesity, Lateral Agency)," *Critical Inquiry* 33, no. 4 (2007): 754.

49. WHO, *Noncommunicable Diseases*, Country Profiles, 2014.

50. Literature on the relationship between beef consumption and these factors is abundant. See, for example, D. Aune, G. Ursin, and M. B. Veierød, "Meat Consumption and the Risk of Type 2 Diabetes: A Systematic Review and Meta-analysis of Cohort Studies," *Diabetologia* 52, no. 11 (2009): 2277–2287; A. M. Bernstein, Q. Sun, F. B. Hu, M. J. Stampfer, J. E. Manson, and W. C. Willett, "Major Dietary Protein Sources and Risk of Coronary Heart Disease in Women," *Circulation* 122, no. 9 (2010): 876–883.

51. WHO African Health Observatory, *Botswana: Analytic Summary — Noncommunicable Diseases and Conditions*, http://www.aho.afro.who.int/profiles_information/index.php/Botswana:Analytical_summary_-_Non-communicable_diseases_and_conditions. See also Mpho Keetile, Kannan Navaneetham, and Gobopamang Letamo, "Patterns and Determinants of Hypertension in Botswana," *Journal of Public Health* 23 (2015): 311–318.

52. Pauline Dikuelo, "Nearly One-Third of Adults in Botswana Obese — Study," *Mmegi*, 17 March 2015, http://www.mmegi.bw/index.php?aid=49943.

53. I am grateful to Abou Farman for the term "fartopocene."

54. Radhika Govindrajan, "Flatulence," Theorizing the Contemporary, Cultural Anthropology website, 12 July 2016, https://culanth.org/fieldsights/916-flatulence.

55. Tobin J. Hammer, Noah Fierer, Bess Hardwick, Asko Simojoki, Eleanor Slade, Juhani Taponen, Heidi Viljanen, and Tomas Roslin, "Treating Cattle with Antibiotics Affects Greenhouse Gas Emissions, and Microbiota in Dung and Dung Beetles," *Proceedings of the Royal Society B: Biological Sciences* 283, no. 1831 (2016), https://doi.org/10.1098/rspb.2016.0150.

56. Joseph Mbaiwa and Onaletshepho Mbaiwa, "The Effects of Veterinary Fences on Wildlife Populations in the Okavango Delta, Botswana," *International Journal of Wilderness* 12, no. 3 (2006): 17–23.

CHAPTER 3. Roads, Sand, and the Motorized Cow

1. Paul Gilroy, "Driving while Black," in *Car Cultures*, ed. Daniel Miller (Oxford: Berg, 2001), 81–104. See also Aimee Meredith Cox, *Shapeshifters: Black Girls and the Choreography of Citizenship* (Durham, NC: Duke University Press, 2015).

2. Leanne Betasamosake Simpson, remarks made at the 13/13 Uprising Seminar on Standing Rock, Columbia Law School, 12 April 2018, http://blogs.law.columbia.edu/uprising1313/12-13/; Marshall Berman, *All That Is Solid Melts into Air: The Experience of Modernity* (New York: Penguin, 1982); Mike Davis, *City of Quartz: Excavating the Future in Los Angeles* (New York: Verso, 1990); Lewis Mumford, *The Urban Prospect* (New York: Harcourt Brace, 1968), 92–107; Gilroy, "Driving while Black."

3. Government of Botswana, *Selected Statistical Indicators, 1966–2016*, Statistics Botswana, Gaborone, 2016.

4. Department of Roads, Ministry of Transport and Communications, "Botswana Roads — Basic Facts," 2011, http://www.gov.bw/en/Ministries --Authorities/Ministries/Ministry-of-Transport-and-Communications /Departments/Department-of-Roads/Divisions/#fecfdd434b8448a296 e57311ec6c669a.

5. Department of Roads, Ministry of Transport and Communications, "Botswana Roads — Basic Facts."

6. The rate went from 9.9 deaths per 100,000 population to 32.4 deaths per 100,000 population. Miriam Sebogo, Rebecca B. Naumann, Rose A. Rudd, Karen Voetsch, Ann M. Dellinger, and Christopher Ndlovu, "The Impact of Alcohol and Road Traffic Policies on Crash Rates in Botswana, 2004–2011, a Time Series Analysis," *Accident Analysis and Prevention* 70 (2014): 33.

7. Sharon Mathlala, "Son, Daughter, Mother, Perish Hours Apart in Two Accidents," *Monitor Mmegi*, 12 September 2016; "Mystery Deaths Rock Kgari Royal Family," *Midweek Sun*, 14 September 2016.

8. See, for example, the comments on the article "Matsha Students Accident — What We Know," *Mmegi*, 14 November 2015, http://www.mmegi .bw/index.php?aid=55716&dir=2015/november/14. Like this comment: "When a minister can purchase 2 suv's, 2 top of the range Mercediz, 2 LandRovers and 2 Patrols, what dificult for each shool to be furnished with a bus each, other than transporting bana ka di-Truck tsa dikgomo." These are replays of earlier such accidents — like the 2003 crash in which five students perished and dozens were injured: "Students Perish in Open Truck Accident," 15–21 August 2003.

9. Sebogo et al., "The Impact of Alcohol and Road Traffic Policies on Crash Rates in Botswana"; Douglas J. Wiebe, S. Ray, T. Maswabi, C. Kgathi, and C. C. Branas, "Economic Development and Road Traffic Fatalities in Two Neighboring African Nations," *African Journal of Emergency Medicine* 6, no. 2 (2016): 80–86; Motor Vehicle Association Fund Road User

Behavior Survey Report, 2014; M. T. Oladiran and H. Pheko, "Some Implications of Driver Training for Road Accidents in Gaborone," *Accident, Analysis, and Prevention* 27, no. 4 (1995): 583–590; Christopher Mupimpila, "Aspects of Road Safety in Botswana," *Development Southern Africa* 25, no. 4 (2008): 425–435.

10. Sarah Lochlann Jain, "'Dangerous Instrumentality': The Bystander as Subject in Automobility," *Cultural Anthropology* 19, no. 1 (2004): 61–94.

11. Conor Gaffey, "Cameroon: U.S. Compensates Family of Boy Killed by Samantha Power's Motorcade," *Newsweek*, 29 June 2016, http://www .newsweek.com/cameroon-us-compensates-family-boy-killed-saman tha-powers-motorcade-475952.

12. World Health Organization, Global Status Report on Road Safety, 2015.

13. World Health Organization, Global Status Report on Road Safety, 2015.

14. This figure is calculated per 100,000 population. World Health Organization, Global Status Report on Road Safety, 2015.

15. That rate is USD 8,600 in 1985 U.S. dollars. Elizabeth Kopits and Maureen Cropper, "Traffic Fatalities and Economic Growth," *Accident Analysis and Prevention* 37, no. 1 (2005): 169–178.

16. World Health Organization, Global Status Report on Road Safety, 2015. Analysts suggest using the WHO figures for comparisons, but also caution that this data set may offer overestimations of crash rates for the least developed countries, Vietnam and China—cited above are middle income. V. Sauerzapf, A. P. Jones, and R. Haynes, "The Problems in Determining International Road Mortality," *Accident Analysis and Prevention* 42, no. 1 (2010): 492–499.

17. F. K. Winston, C. Rineer, R. Menon, and S. P. Baker, "The Carnage Wrought by Major Economic Change: Ecological Study of Traffic-Related Mortality and the Reunification of Germany," *BMJ* 318, no. 7199 (1999): 1647–1650.

18. For more on trauma care in low- and middle-income countries, see Harris Solomon's new work in India. Harris Solomon, "Shifting Gears: Triage and Traffic in Urban India," *Medical Anthropology Quarterly* 31, no. 3 (2017): 349–364.

19. Terje Peder Hanche-Olsen, Lulseged Alemu, Asgaut Viste, Torben Wisborg, and Kari S. Hansen, "Trauma Care in Africa: A Status Report from Botswana, Guided by the World Health Organization's 'Guidelines for Essential Trauma Care,'" *World Journal of Surgery* 36, no. 10 (2012): 2371–2383.

20. Kenda Mutongi, *Matatu: A History of Popular Transportation in Nairobi* (Chicago: University of Chicago Press, 2017).

21. Jain, "'Dangerous Instrumentality'"; see also Mark Lamont, "Accidents Have No Cure! Road Death as Industrial Catastrophe in Eastern Africa," *African Studies* 71, no. 2 (2012): 174–194.

22. Jain, "'Dangerous Instrumentality.'"

23. This is similar to William Cronon's argument about the railroads in nineteenth-century Chicago. William Cronon, *Nature's Metropolis: Chicago and the Great West* (New York: W. W. Norton, 1991).

24. Isaac Schapera notes how, in 1889, the Ngwaketse chief Bathoen I "'stuck up a notice on the roadside at the entrance' to his capital (Kanye), informing 'my people, and all other people, that no wagons shall enter or leave' the town on Sunday; that notice was worded in Tswana, Dutch, and English (Bent 1892: 643)." Isaac Schapera, *Tribal Innovators: Tswana Chiefs and Social Change, 1795–1940*, LSE Monographs in Social Anthropology (London: Athlone, 1970).

25. Barbara Ntombi Ngwenya, "The Development of Transport Infrastructure in the Bechuanaland Protectorate 1885–1966," *Botswana Notes and Records* 16 (1984): 78. See the photograph of the huge "workparty of women summoned by the chief to clean the dam in Mochudi," in John L. Comaroff, Jean Comaroff, and Deborah James, eds., *Picturing a Colonial Past: The African Photographs of Isaac Schapera* (Chicago: University of Chicago Press, 2007), 190.

26. Schapera, *Tribal Innovators*, 97.

27. Schapera, *Tribal Innovators*, 152.

28. Ornulf Gulbrandsen, *The State and the Social: State Formation in Botswana* (New York: Berghahn, 2013), 84.

29. Ngwenya, "The Development of Transport Infrastructure in the Bechuanaland Protectorate 1885–1966," 77.

30. Jan-Bart Gewald, "Missionaries, Herero, and Motorcars: Mobility and the Impact of Motor Vehicles in Namibia Before 1940," *International Journal of African Historical Studies* 35, nos. 2–3 (2002): 257–285.

31. R. T. McCutcheon, "The Main Findings of the District Pilot Project of Labour-Intensive Road Construction and Maintenance in Botswana and the Implications for Similar Projects in South Africa," *Development Southern Africa* 8, no. 2 (1991): 149–170.

32. Now, of course, in the United States, prison labor is used to fight wildfires.

33. David Livingstone, *Missionary Travels in South Africa* (London: John Murray, 1857):121, cited in Schapera, *Tribal Innovators*, 160.

34. Tesfaye Teklu, "The Prevention and Mitigation of Famine: Policy Lessons from Botswana and Sudan," *Disasters* 18, no. 1 (1994): 35–47; Onalenna Selolwane, "Welfare, Social Protection, and Poverty Reduction," in *Poverty Reduction and Changing Policy Regimes in Botswana*, ed. Onalenna Selolwane (New York: Palgrave Macmillan / United Nations Institute for Social Development, 2012), 102–138; R. T. McCutcheon, "The Botswana District Roads Labour-Intensive Improvement and Maintenance Programme—a Summary," *Development Southern Africa* 5, no. 3 (1988): 387.

35. Selolwane, "Welfare, Social Protection, and Poverty Reduction," 106.

36. McCutcheon, "The Botswana District Roads," 387.

37. I am grateful to Jackie Solway for this observation.

38. Teklu, "The Prevention and Mitigation of Famine," 38.

39. Selolwane, "Welfare, Social Protection, and Poverty Reduction," 130.

40. Teklu, "The Problem and Mitigation of Famine," 42–43.

41. Kesitegile S. M. Gobotswang, "Poverty Alleviation Strategies in Botswana: The Case of Labour-Intensive Public Works Programme," *Botswana Notes and Records* 36 (2004): 27–36.

42. Margaret Buchanan-Smith and Gabolekwe Tlogelang, "Linking Relief and Development: A Case Study of Botswana," *IDS Bulletin* 25, no. 4 (1994): 56.

43. Selolwane, "Welfare, Social Protection, and Poverty Reduction,"130.

44. Dithapelo Lefoko Keorapetse and Segomotso Masegonyana Keakopa, "Records Management as a Means to Fighting Corruption and Enhancing Accountability in Botswana," *ESARBICA Journal: Journal of the Eastern and Southern Branch of the International Council on Archives* 31 (2012); Monkagedi Gaotlhabogwa, "BDPs Financiers Paraded," *Mmegi*, 21 November 2011, http://www.mmegi.bw/index.php?sid=1&aid=91&dir=2011/November/Monday21.

45. Bame Piet, "The Rot on Our Roads" *Mmegi*, 28 September 2012, http://www.mmegi.bw/index.php?sid=1&aid=43&dir=2012%2FSeptember%2FFriday28&fb_comment_id=502338726443059_9935375S; "Roads Department Falls under Multiple Probes," *Sunday Standard*, 24 September 2012, http://www.sundaystandard.info/roads-dept-falls-under-multiple-probe.

46. Bame Piet, "Corruption Court Worsens Judicial Delays," *Mmegi*, 17 October 2014, https://bw.newshub.org/corruption-court-worsens-judicial-delays-5054428.html#.

47. "Government Blows a Billion in Project Cost Overruns," *Botswana Gazette*, 7 July 2016, http://www.thegazette.news/?p=15387.

48. Botswana Roads Department, Ministry of Transport and Communications, "Public Notice: Progress Status on Roads Projects under Construction and Maintenance," 2011.

49. "The Road to Hell Paved with Billions of Pula," *Sunday Standard*, 12 September 2010, http://www.sundaystandard.info/road-hell-paved-billions-pula; Brian Benza, "Kang-Hukuntsi Road Halts as Sinohydro Demands Payment," *Mmegi*, 25 May 2012, http://www.mmegi.bw/index.php?sid=4&aid=486&dir=2012/May/Friday25/.

50. "Kang-Hukuntsi Road Behind Schedule," *Botswana Daily News*, 21 December 2010, http://www.gov.bw/en/News/Kang-Hukuntsi-Road/.

51. Petroleum is a vast and militarized system. Timothy Mitchell, *Carbon Democracy: Political Power in the Age of Oil* (New York: Verso, 2013).

52. Mieka Ritsema, "Gaborone Is Growing Like a Baby: Life Expectancies and Death Expectancies," *Africa Development* 33, no. 3 (2008): 81–108.

53. Edward Allen and Joseph Iano, *Fundamentals of Building Construction: Materials and Methods*, 5th ed. (Hoboken, NJ: John Wiley, 2009), cited by Paul Kinanawa Lyamuya and Kazi Nurul Alam, "Earth Construction in Botswana: Reviving and Improving the Tradition," paper presented at the Commonwealth Association of Architects, 20th General Assembly and Conference, Dhaka (Bangladesh), 2013.

54. Vince Beiser, "He Who Controls the Sand: Kenya's 'Mining Mafias,'" *Guardian*, 1 March 2017.

55. David Owen, "The End of Sand," *New Yorker*, 29 May 2017, http://www.newyorker.com/magazine/2017/05/29/the-world-is-running-out-of-sand.

56. *The Use of Kgalagadi Sands in Road Construction* (Gaborone: Roads Department, Ministry of Transport and Communications, Botswana, 2010), 20.

57. UNEP Global Environmental Alert Service, "Sand, Rarer Than One Thinks," March 2014, 3.

58. Beiser, "He Who Controls the Sand"; Vince Beiser, "The Deadly Global War for Sand," *Wired*, 26 March 2015.

59. Alpha M. Tshwenyego and Richard Poulin, "Mineral Aggregate Production in Botswana," *International Journal of Surface Mining, Reclamation, and Environment* 11, no. 3 (1997): 129–134; Zeph Kajevu, "Illegal Sand Mining to Negative River Eco-systems," *Sunday Standard*, 22 September 2013, http://www.sundaystandard.info/illegal-sand-mining-negative-river-eco-systems.

60. As Deborah Durham observes, when concrete became the basic building material in Botswana, replacing mud blocks for housing in the 1990s, villagers also began digging in local riverbeds; or, if they lacked transport to haul this excavated sand, they might simply dig out of the sand roads in the village, thereby making them impassable for cars (perhaps eventually giving impetus to tarring). Deborah Durham, "Cars vs. Houses: Moral Choices in Middle-Income Botswana," *Africa* forthcoming.

61. Ministry of Minerals, Energy, and Water Resources, "River Sand Mining Has Negative Environmental Impacts," 27 February 2015, http://www.gov.bw/en/Ministries—Authorities/Ministries/Ministry-of-Minerals-Energy-and-Water-Resources-MMWER/News-and-Press-Releases/SAND-MINING-HAS-NEGATIVE-ENVIRONMENTAL-IMPACTS/.

62. UNEP Global Environmental Alert Service, "Sand, Rarer Than One Thinks," 3, 4–5.

63. *The Use of Kgalagadi Sand in Road Construction*; African Community Access Programme, "Guideline on the Use of Sand in Road Construction in the SADC Region" (Association of Southern African Road Agencies, May 2013).

64. Mitchell, *Carbon Democracy*; Ed Kashi and Michael Watts, eds.,

Curse of the Black Gold: 50 Years of Oil in the Niger Delta (Brooklyn: Power-house Books, 2010).

65. "Job Losses Follow Hyundai Liquidation," IRIN, 18 January 2000, http://www.irinnews.org/report/11782/south-africa-job-losses-follow -hyundai-liquidation.

66. "Botswana Car Plant Goes Cheap," *Car Magazine*, 13 September 2001, http://www.carmag.co.za/news_post/botswana-car-plant-goes -cheap/.

67. "Businessman, Two Workers Die in Accident," *Herald* (Harare), 18 January 2008.

68. Mira Langer, "Rautenbach Served with Hyundai Papers at Selebi Trial," *Mail and Guardian*, 19 November 2009, https://mg.co.za/article /2009-11-19-rautenbach-served-with-hyundai-papers-at-selebi-trial; Branko Brkic, "The Selebi Saga: Selebi Laughs as Agliotti Sheds Tears," *Daily Maverick*, 9 October 2009, https://www.dailymaverick.co.za/arti cle/2009-10-09-the-selebi-saga-selebi-laughs-as-agliotti-sheds-tears/# .WZ4bb5N94Wo.

69. The names of Rautenbach's companies have changed and prolifer-ated over time. Chris McGreal, "The Motiveless Murder and Napoleon of Africa," *Guardian*, 15 December 1999, https://www.theguardian.com /world/1999/dec/16/chrismcgreal.

70. McGreal, "The Motiveless Murder."

71. "US Billionaire New Johnny Come Lately into ZANU-PF Dark World," *Zimbabwe Daily*, 16 June 2011, https://www.thezimbabwedaily .com/news/8355-us-billionaire-new-johnny-come-lately-into-zanu-pf -dark-world.html?doing_wp_cron=1503450721.2299759387969970703125; McGreal, "The Motiveless Murder."

72. When Rautenbach abandoned the first proposed ethanol site in Masvingo due to a lack of water, the Zimbabwean government courted Saadi Qaddafi, son of then Libyan president Muammar, with discussion of a new dam. With Qaddafi soon out of the game, eventually it seems Mugabe took over this site. Lauren van der Westhuizen, "Qaddafi's Son Is Considering Investing in Dam, Ethanol Project in Zimbabwe," Bloom-berg News, 25 August 2010, reposted on Commercial Farmers Union of Zimbabwe website, http://www.cfuzim.org/index.php/agriculture/868 -qaddafis-son-is-considering-investing-in-dam-ethinol-project-in-zimba bwe.

73. "All Eyes on Zimbabwe's Ethanol," *Africa Report*, 21 October 2013, http://www.theafricareport.com/Southern-Africa/all-eyes-on-zimbabw es-ethanol.html; Ian Scoones, Blasio Mavedzenge, and Felix Murimba-rimba, "Sugar, People and Politics in Zimbabwe's Lowveld," *Journal of Southern African Studies* 43, no. 3 (2017): 567–584; Lance Guma, "Mliswa Exposes Rautenbach and ZANU PF Patronage," *Zimbabwean*, 3 Septem-ber 2012, http://www.thezimbabwean.co/2012/09/mliswa-exposes-raut enbach-and-zanu/.

74. Patience Mutopo and Manase Chiweshe, "Large Scale Land Deals, Global Capital and the Politics of Livelihoods: Experiences of Women Small-Holder Farmers in Chisumbanje, Zimbabwe," paper presented at the International Conference on Global Land Grabbing II, October 17–19, 2012, Department of Development Sociology, Cornell University.

75. "Strike Hits Zimbabwe's Sole Ethanol Producer Green Fuel," *New Zimbabwe*, 12 May 2015, https://www.newzimbabwe.com/strike-hits-zimbabwes-sole-ethanol-producer-green-fuel/.

76. Michael Hobbes, "The Untouchables: Why It's Getting Harder to Stop Multinational Corporations," *Foreign Policy*, 11 April 2016, http://foreignpolicy.com/2016/04/11/the-untouchables-zimbabwe-green-fuel-multinational-corporations/.

77. Veneranda Langa, "Green Fuel Told to Compensate Villagers," *Standard*, 22 February 2015, https://www.thestandard.co.zw/2015/02/22/green-fuel-told-compensate-villagers/; Andrew Mambondiyani, "Amid Epic Drought, Villagers Bitter over Zimbabwean Ethanol Plant," *Mongabay*, 28 July 2016, https://news.mongabay.com/2016/07/amid-epic-drought-villagers-bitter-over-zimbabwean-ethanol-plant/; Hobbes, "The Untouchables."

78. Samuel Kadungure, "22 Perish in Ethanol Inferno," *Herald*, 31 October 2013, http://www.herald.co.zw/22-perish-in-ethanol-inferno/.

79. Jim Lane, "Biofuels Mandates around the World: 2016," *Biofuels Digest*, 3 January 2016, http://www.biofuelsdigest.com/bdigest/2016/01/03/biofuels-mandates-around-the-world-2016/.

80. Joseph Fargione, Jason Hill, David Tilman, Stephen Polasky, and Peter Hawthorne, "Land Clearing and the Biofuel Carbon Debt," *Science* 319, no. 5867 (2008): 1235–1238, doi: 10.1126/science.1152747. This situation is not unlike how cattle feed is in tension with crops for domestic consumption.

81. Deepak Rajagopal and David Zilberman, "Review of Environmental, Economic and Policy Aspects of Biofuels," *Policy Research Working Paper Number 4341* (World Bank, Development Research Group, September 2007). Corn seems particularly problematic: C. Ford Runge, "The Case against More Ethanol: It's Simply Bad for Environment," Yale Environment 360, 25 May 2016, http://e360.yale.edu/features/the_case_against_ethanol_bad_for_environment; Mark Jackobson, "Effects of Ethanol (E85) versus Gasoline Vehicles on Cancer and Mortality in the United States," Environmental Science and Technology 41, no. 11 (2007): 4150–4157. Brazil's sugarcane biofuel does better until one takes land clearance into account.

82. Patience Mutopo and Manase Chiweshe, "Water Resources and Biofuel Production after the Fast-Track Land Reform in Zimbabwe," *African Identities* 12, no. 1 (2014): 124–138.

83. Song Jung-a, Christian Oliver, and Tom Burgis, "Daewoo to Cul-

tivate Madagascar Land for Free," *Financial Times*, 19 November 2008, https://www.ft.com/content/6e894c6a-b65c-11dd-89dd-0000779fd18c; "The Madagascar Model," *Economist*, 13 November 2009, http://www .economist.com/node/14742547; Julian Ryall and Mike Pfanz, "Land Rental Deal Collapses after Backlash against 'Colonialism,'" *Telegraph*, 14 January 2009, http://www.telegraph.co.uk/news/worldnews/africaan dindianocean/madagascar/4240955/Land-rental-deal-collapses-after -backlash-against-colonialism.html.

84. Tsaone Basimanebotlhe, "GCC Meets on Rampant, Roaming Livestock," *Mmegi* 6 January 2016, http://www.mmegi.bw/index.php?aid=56 754&dir=2016/january/06.

85. Durham, "Cars vs. Houses."

86. Mbongeni Mguni, "Working Hours to Be Staggered as Vehicle Numbers Explode," *Mmegi*, 9 November 2012, http://www.mmegi.bw /index.php?sid=4&aid=210&dir=2012/November/Friday9.

87. Aubrey Lute, "Remember That Botswana Doesn't Make Cars So Imports Are the Way," *Weekend Post*, 31 July 2017, http://www.weekendpost .co.bw/wp-news-details.php?nid=4116.

88. Tshepo Bogosing, "Dealers Complain over Japanese Car Imports," *Mmegi*, 9 February 2005, https://www.mmegi.bw/2005/February/Wed nesday9/123583538933.html.

89. Bester Gabotlale, "Difong-Kong Rule, Local Cars Get a Battering," *Mmegi*, 27 October 2006, http://www.mmegi.bw/2006/October/Friday 27/997635942689.html.

90. Boniface Keakabetse, "Japanese Cars Fuel Global Warming— Mokaila," *Mmegi*, 29 July 2011; Arnold Letsholo, "Gaborone's Pollution Peaks in Winter—UB Professor," *Mmegi*, 8 August 2011.

91. Letsholo, "Gaborone's Pollution Peaks in Winter."

92. John Makhutjisa Motshetja, "Let the Customer Decide," letter to the editor, *Mmegi*, 24 February 2005, https://www.mmegi.bw/2005/Feb ruary/Thursday24/597874212321.html.

93. Wanetshe Mosinyi, "Japanese Vehicle Exports to Botswana to Increase," *Mmegi*, 3 March 2009, http://www.mmegi.bw/index.php?sid =4&aid=13&dir=2009/March/Tuesday3.

94. See comments at https://www.facebook.com/MmegiOnline /posts/10154030985141824.

95. "Myanmar Tops a List Ranking Japan's Used Cars Export," Japan International Freight Forwarders Association, Inc., 2 February 2015, https://www.jiffa.or.jp/en/news/entry-3330.html; "Japan Vehicle Export Statistics," JEVIC, http://jevic.com/import-and-export/importing -exporting-from-japan/statistics/.

96. "The Recycling of End-of-Life Vehicles in Japan," *jfs Newsletter*, no. 50, October 2006, http://www.japanfs.org/en/news/archives/news_id 027816.html.

97. Andrew Pollack, "Why the Cars in Japan Look Just Like New," *New York Times*, 12 September 1993, http://www.nytimes.com/1993/09/12/world/why-the-cars-in-japan-look-just-like-new.html?mcubz=1.

98. James Brook, "Japan's Used Cars Find New Lives on Russian Roads," *New York Times*, 12 February 2003, http://www.nytimes.com/2003/02/12/business/japan-s-used-cars-find-new-lives-on-russian-roads.html?mcubz=1.

99. Rob de Jong, *Exporting Pollution: Dumping Dirty Fuels and Vehicles in Africa* (Transport Unit at UN Environment, 15 September 2016).

100. De Jong, *Exporting Pollution*.

101. Chris Obore, "Radioactive Japanese Cars on the Market," *Monitor*, 26 August 2012, http://www.monitor.co.ug/News/National/Radioactive-Japanese-cars-on-the-market/688334-1487016-suvsj8/index.html; Julian Ryall, "Japanese Dealers Selling 'Radioactive Cars,'" *Telegraph*, 26 October 2011, http://www.telegraph.co.uk/news/worldnews/asia/japan/8849664/Japanese-dealers-selling-radioactive-cars.html.

102. Obore, "Radioactive Japanese Cars on the Market."

103. "Radioactive Cars from Japan Arrive in Chilean Port," Associated Press, 2 May 2011.

104. "Japanese Vehicle Inspection Firm Blacklisted for Shoddy Radiation Test," *Standard*, 13 September 2015, https://www.standardmedia.co.ke/business/article/2000176155/japanese-vehicle-inspection-firm-blacklisted-for-shoddy-radiation-test.

105. "Radioactive Cars from Japan Keep Turning Up in Central Asia," *AutoWeek*, 10 July 2014, http://autoweek.com/article/car-news/radioactive-cars-japan-keep-turning-central-asia.

106. Bert Wilkinson, "Radioactive Cars from Japan Turning Up in Caribbean," *Amsterdam News*, 16 January 2014, http://amsterdamnews.com/news/2014/jan/16/radioactive-cars-japan-turning-caribbean/.

107. "Banks Encourage Consumption," *Botswana Daily News*, 4 August 2006. This figure compares with the 560 million pula made in business loans.

108. Paulene Dikuelo, "Batswana Swamped in Debt—Microlender," *Mmegi*, 24 June 2015, http://www.mmegi.bw/index.php?aid=52131&dir=2015/june/24.

109. Julie Livingston, "Suicide, Risk, and Investment in the Heart of the African Miracle," *Cultural Anthropology* 24, no. 4 (2009): 652–680.

110. Catherine Lutz, "The U.S. Car Colossus and the Production of Inequality," *American Ethnologist* 41, no. 2 (2014): 232–245.

CHAPTER 4. Power and Possibility

Epigraphs: Lauren Olamina, "Earthseed: The Books of the Living," in Octavia Butler, *Parable of the Sower* (New York: Grand Central Publishing, 1993). "Our country is gone. It has been eaten by the clever ones," Sessio

Man, 2013 (translation mine). This reader comment appeared in response to a 2013 news report that Botswana had issued prospecting licenses in the Kalahari for natural gas exploration.

1. Pierre du Plessis, "Gathering the Kalahari: Tracks, Trails, and More-Than-Human Landscapes" (PhD dissertation, Aarhus University and University of California–Santa Cruz joint program, 2018); Pierre du Plessis, "Geomorphological Resistance: Temporal Disjuncture and the Violence of Shale-Gas Prospecting," draft chapter, n.d.

2. Matteo Albano, Marco Polcari, Christian Bignami, Marco Moro, Michele Saroli, and Salvatore Stramondo, "Did Anthropogenic Activities Trigger the 3 April 2017 M_w 6.5 Botswana Earthquake?," *Remote Sensing* 9, no. 10 1028 (2017), https://doi.org/10.3390/rs9101028.

3. "Press Statement on So-Called Fracking Activities in Botswana—19 November 2013," reproduced in Sharon Mathala, "Controversy Erupts over Fracking in the CKGR," *Mmegi*, 20 November 2013, http://www.mmegi.bw/index.php?aid=3865&fb_comment_id=598080280245575_5607138#fe5b718fc725c4.

4. This study suggests that salinity levels vary depending on a range of factors including the age of the water in the aquifer and the depth of the coal bed. National Academies of Sciences, Engineering, and Medicine, *Management and Effects of Coalbed Methane Produced Water in the Western United States*, Consensus study report (Washington, DC: National Academies Press, 2010), https://www.nap.edu/catalog/12915/management-and-effects-of-coalbed-methane-produced-water-in-the-western-united-states.

5. United States Environmental Protection Agency, Office of Water, *Coalbed Methane Extraction: Detailed Study Report*, EPA-820-R-10-022 (Washington, DC: EPA, 2010).

6. Thomas W. Pearson, "How Fracking's Appetite for Sand Is Devouring Rural Communities," *Sapiens*, 4 May 2018, https://www.sapiens.org/culture/fracking-rural-wisconsin/.

7. Jeff Barbee, Mira Dutschke, and David Smith, "Botswana Faces Questions over Licenses for Fracking Companies in Kalahari," *Guardian*, 17 November 2013, https://www.theguardian.com/environment/2013/nov/18/botswana-accusations-fracking-kalahari.

8. Anita Powell, "Botswana Admits to Fracking after Documentary," *Voice of America News*, 21 November 2013, https://www.voanews.com/a/botswana-admits-to-allowing-fracking-after-documentary/1794790.html.

9. Jeff Barbee, "Botswana Sells Fracking Rights in National Park," *Guardian*, 2 December 2015, https://www.theguardian.com/environment/2015/dec/02/botswana-sells-fracking-rights-in-national-park.

10. See, for example, Jacqueline Solway, "Human Rights and NGO 'Wrongs': Conflict Diamonds, Culture Wars and the 'Bushman Ques-

tion,'" *Africa* 79, no. 3 (2009): 321–346; Edwin Wilmsen, *Land Filled with Flies: A Political Economy of the Kalahari* (Chicago: University of Chicago Press, 1989).

11. Kenneth Good, "Authoritarian Liberalism: A Defining Characteristic of Botswana," *Journal of Contemporary African Studies* 14, no. 1 (1996): 29–51.

12. Du Plessis, "Geomorphological Resistance."

13. This concept of the "rightful share" is best articulated by James Ferguson, *Give a Man a Fish: Reflections on the New Politics of Distribution* (Durham, NC: Duke University Press, 2015).

14. Erin Brodwin, "A New Analysis Suggests Hurricane Harvey Caused 4.6 Million Pounds of Chemicals to Be Released—but the Risk Is Still Unclear," *Business Insider*, 12 September 2017, http://www.businessinsider .com/oil-refineries-hit-harvey-releasing-chemicals-pollutants-2017-8.

15. Anna Lowenhaupt Tsing, *The Mushroom at the End of the World: On the Possibility of Life in Capitalist Ruins* (Princeton, NJ: Princeton University Press, 2015). I find great inspiration and comfort in the work of landscape architect Kate Orff, who along with her colleagues at SCAPE and the communities with whom she works is creating new kinds of growth (https://www.scapestudio.com/about/). Many others are out there. New growth is possible.

INDEX